C-1

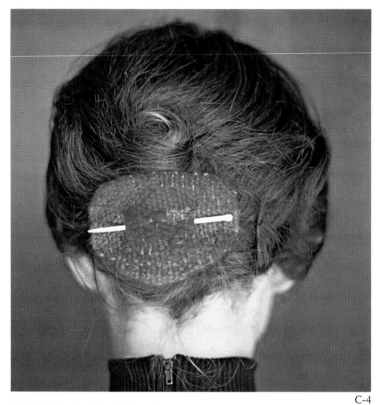

C-4

C-2

C-3

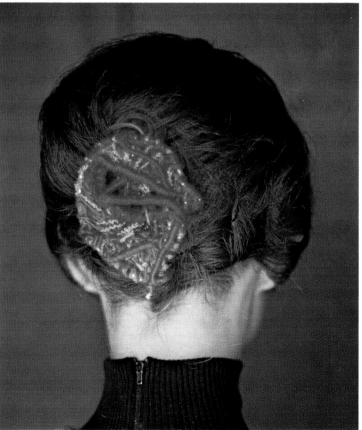

C-5

C-7

C-8

C-9

C-10

C-11

C-12

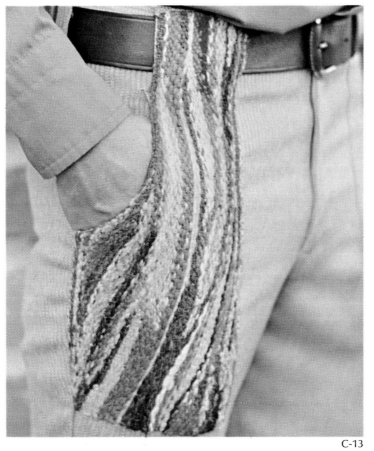

C-13

C-14

shaped weaving

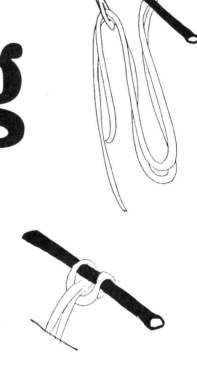

MAKING GARMENTS
AND ACCESSORIES WITH
SIMPLE NEEDLE- AND
FINGER-WEAVING
TECHNIQUES

NIK KREVITSKY
LOIS ERICSON

VAN NOSTRAND REINHOLD COMPANY
New York Cincinnati Toronto London Melbourne

Books by Nik Krevitsky

Batik: Art and Craft
Stitchery: Art and Craft
Shaped Weaving: Making Garments and Accessories with Simple Needle- and Finger-Weaving Techniques *(with Lois Ericson)*

Captions for Color Photos

C-1. The pin-woven poncho, of which this is a detail, was created by Diane Ericson, who models it on the front cover.

C-2. The pendant was woven with wire on a wire form.

C-3. Both pendant and earring were woven with wire and fuzzy yarn.

C-4. The barrette was woven on a pin loom and with a slit tapestry technique for the hairpin.

C-5. Wrapped threads enhance the design of this barrette.

C-6. Lois Ericson wears a neckpiece woven of white flax, brown rayon and green wool and accented with feathers.

C-7. Wrapped yarns decorate a neckpiece that shows how weaving may be attached to leather.

C-8. This pendant has a shaped copper wire framework.

C-9. Flexible metallic thread is part of the weaving in this pendant.

C-10. Braided fringe and beads were added to the finger-woven purse.

C-11. A woven sleeve can be attached to a dress.

C-12. The neckpiece was made on a cardboard pin loom.

C-13. A woven patch pocket covers the slack pocket.

C-14. The patriotic bolero vest was woven with heavy wool on a pin loom.

C-15. The finger-woven body ornament, created by Vinnie Hinz, has a chevron design.

Black and white photographs by Michael A. Hurwitz
Drawings by Diane Ericson

Except when otherwise credited, all depicted articles are the work of the authors:

Lois Ericson — Figs. 1, 6, 17, 33, 62, 64, 65, 72, 73, 74, 77, 88, 89, 90, 91, 92, 93, 101, 102, 104, 106, 107, 108, 109, 110, 112, 117, 118, 133, 135, 137, 153, 161, 167.

Nik Krevitsky — Figs. 4, 5, 10, 21, 23, 28, 29, 59, 61, 75, 76, 86, 87, 99, 121, 130, 140, 141, 142, 144, 148, 149, 150, 151, 152, 154, 155, 156, 157.

Van Nostrand Reinhold Company Regional Offices:
New York Cincinnati Chicago Millbrae Dallas
Van Nostrand Reinhold Co. International Offices:
London Toronto Melbourne

Copyright © 1974 by Litton Educational Publishing, Inc.
Library of Congress Catalog Card Number: 73-16704
ISBN: 0 442-22321-8 paper
ISBN: 0 442-22324-2 cloth

Published by Van Nostrand Reinhold Company
A Division of Litton Educational Publishing, Inc.
450 West 33rd Street, New York, N.Y. 10001

16 15 14 13 12 10 9 8 7 6 5 4 3 2 1

Library of Congress Cataloging in Publication Data

Krevitsky, Nik.
  Shaped weaving.

  Bibliography: p.
  1. Hand weaving. 2. Clothing and dress.
3. Dress accessories. I. Ericson, Lois, joint author. II. Title.
TT848.K68   746.9'2   73–16704
ISBN 0–442–22324–2
ISBN 0–442–22321–8 (pbk.)

Part I: Techniques

Part II: Examples

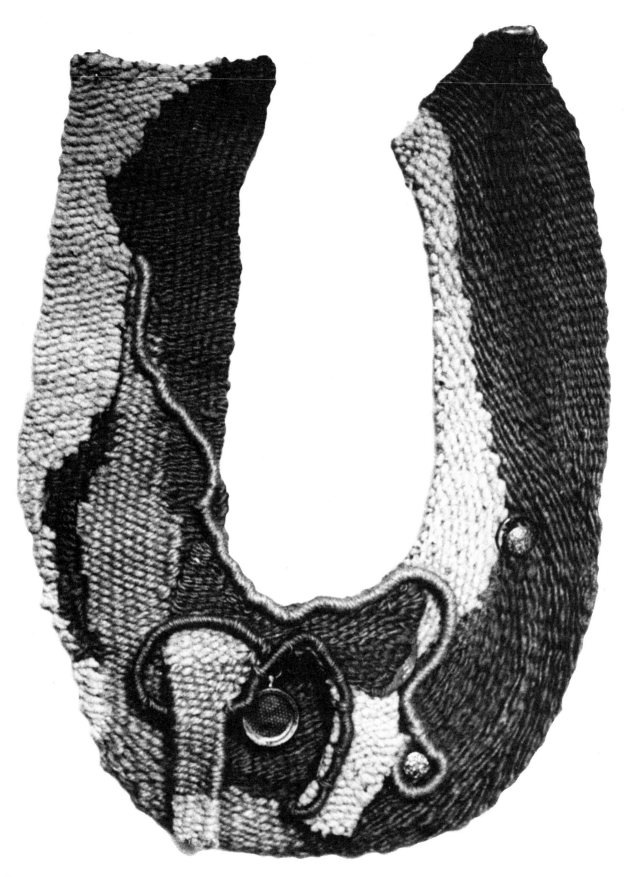

Introduction

If you have never done any weaving, the entire process might seem overwhelming. The thought of threading a complicated loom and of all the time involved in preparation for the weaving might easily intimidate any beginner. If, however, you are presented with the prospect of a simple device which anyone can make, thread and weave upon within just a few minutes' time, you have already cleared the first hurdle. There is no mystery to the technique.

Arranging for the weaving is as simple as stretching a thread back and forth over a pin framework or a notched cardboard shape. The actual weaving in and out is nothing more than the simple operation of alternating a threaded needle between these stretched threads which have become your warp. Your only concern is to interlock the weaving threads by going over and under the warp in some regular fashion. If you are careful at the end or edges, there will be no problem of finishing off the weaving. You have a completed object when you remove the pins or slip the form off the notched cardboard. There is nothing more to do except to add decorative elements if you desire, or findings such as hooks and eyes if necessary.

Although needle weaving on cardboard looms goes more slowly than passing a shuttle through rows quickly opened in two-harness looms, it has more versatility. You can form various shapes and you can change your direction of working. Also, you can work anywhere on the piece, see the entire object all at once, and are not restricted to working row after row progressively. The weaving may be done in a meandering way, and many other variations not possible on treadle looms may be employed. One other great advantage is the minimal equipment and tools needed. You make your own loom from commonly available material — cardboard and straight pins — which you are likely to have around the house. The only essential weaving tool is a large-eyed blunt-end needle, preferably with a curved tip.

Facing page: 1. An example of needle weaving on a cardboard loom.

Although no previous knowledge of weaving or any related techniques is necessary, you probably will get going faster if you are accustomed to any of the hand arts that use fiber, especially needlework.

This book will explore elementary techniques of needle and finger weaving, with an emphasis on making shaped objects you can wear and accessories for clothing. In Part I, several nonloom and simple cardboard loom techniques are presented, including the method for making irregular forms with finger weaving. The techniques are simple, and any individual can make these shaped forms to suit his desire or need.

In Part II, we will show a wide array of shaped forms for dress, including collars and necklaces, vests, capes, and parts of garments, such as insets, sleeves, yokes, appliqués, pockets, cuffs, emblems, as well as separate objects like jewelry, bags and hats. These objects are sometimes shown combined with other materials and we also include examples requiring the use of related techniques in addition to the simple tapestry weaving on cardboard looms and shaped finger-weaving, the two techniques to which we devote most of our attention. Since there are so many sources available at all the different levels for learning these other techniques, we have not analyzed or presented them step by step. Many books on macramé, knitting, crochet and basic weaving techniques are to be found, and we have listed some personal recommendations in the Bibliography for further reference.

2. Anita Allen models a chevron finger-woven body ornament. (See also Figure 40 and color photo C-15).

We hope that the knowledge that he can create with freedom from the beginning will make the reader eager to start. Even young children can make exciting objects with these elementary techniques, and anyone can create his own simple design.

Perhaps the most surprising aspect of nonloom weaving is the variety of possibilities it presents, and the design and technical innovations that the beginner can bring to it. Once you get started, you will find many easy ways to make many things, and you will soon discover your own special style.

In the following pages we will demonstrate the techniques for cardboard and nonloom weaving, provide many examples of their application and also offer numerous further ideas. What you do with these ideas — how you apply, develop, or expand them — is up to you. There are no set patterns or rules to follow, although we do outline some step-by-step methods as a suggestion of ways to begin and to overcome hurdles.

We want to stress that it is important to experiment. A free, unhampered attitude will turn your first attempts into revelations and should persuade you that following your personal taste will yield satisfying results. All you need in order to begin is some yarn, a needle, some pins, scissors and a piece of cardboard — plus the desire to explore and experiment, and the courage to get started. Now the adventure begins.

Part I: Techniques

Surface Weaving or Darning

One of the simplest means of achieving a shaped form is through surface weaving. It is done by laying in a series of parallel threads on the surface of a fabric; stitching these threads close together back and forth creates a framework for the weaving in and out in the other direction. Needle weaving across the warp fills in the form. When you have finished, the warp and weft will be indistinguishable one from the other.

Undoubtedly familiar to many readers, this procedure is often used to add strength to worn areas of a fabric, or to cover a hole, and in such cases is frequently referred to as "darning." But darning can be decorative as well as functional; the teen-age craze for embellishing blue jeans and other garments with darning proves this.

3. This surface-woven floral design was made with assorted yarns on woolen fabric.

Since surface weaving is a more direct method of making patches than with pin-loom weaving, we suggest that you begin this way. For your first exercise, start on a strong, yet open-weave base fabric. If the shape you plan is intricate or figurative, it might help for you to draw it first on the base fabric with tailor's chalk or a felt pen. The direction of your framework lines (or warp) depends upon the design. The lines do not all have to be parallel. They may fan out or change direction.

Below, left: 4. A detail of Figure 3 shows how the weaving is attached to the base fabric.
Below, right: 5. After parallel threads of varying length have been stitched onto the base fabric to become warp, needle weaving in and out on these threads fills in the form. In this example, the same thick and thin yarns are being used for both warp and weft.

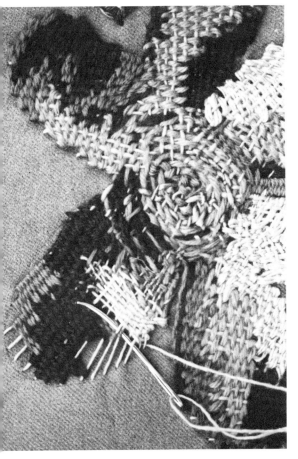

Cardboard Looms

Many simple looms may be made on cardboard. Among them are pin-, notched-, slit- and stitch-edge varieties. Each provides a slightly different way of working and you may soon discover a preference for one after trying the others. If pins are used, you will want a surface soft enough to push the pins into easily. When notches are used you will need edges which can be cut with scissors. This also applies to the material for the slit-edge technique. Stitch-edge looms are more easily made with thin flexible cardboard than with corrugated material.

There are many possibilities and considerations depending upon the way you work and the specific materials and tools you have available. You might prefer fine brads or other headless nails to pins, in which case you may need a wooden surface, such as ¼" plywood, and of course a hammer. Whatever your choice and style of working you will find these simple looms challenging and rewarding.

The Pin Loom Pin-loom weaving is the simple technique that was used for many of the examples illustrated in this book. Like all the methods we talk about in this book, the advantages of this technique are the availability of equipment, the small cost of the materials, and the simplicity of the method. It is an excellent way for you to achieve a shaped piece, and you can form any shape you like. There are no edges to finish, no warp threads to fasten or weave in; the object is complete as woven when you remove it from its one-of-a-kind loom.

The loom surface should be rigid — you can use a piece of sturdy cardboard or possibly a corrugated cardboard box — and at least an inch larger on all sides than the size of the object you plan to make. Another excellent surface is a piece of indoor-outdoor carpeting glued to a piece of fiberboard or heavy cardboard; this base provides a firm working surface, and the pins stay in well. Corkboard is also suitable, as is styrofoam. You will be wise to keep your background color neutral and the surface plain rather than decorated, since your work will be seen against it.

You can draw the shape in pencil or felt-tip pen directly on the cardboard. With other surfaces, we recommend a cut-out pattern; cut out the shape of the object you wish to weave on plain paper, such as shelf or wrapping paper. Until you have become familiar with this method of weaving, your first efforts should be fairly simple shapes, such as small objects suitable as ornaments or a pocket. Once you are set up for the weaving, you can easily complete your first pin-loom project in one short session. After cutting out the design, place the cut-paper pattern on the cardboard. You are now ready to make the loom and then to warp it. You create the pin-loom around your pattern.

The first important step in beginning your weaving on this type of loom is the warping, or preparation of the pin loom.

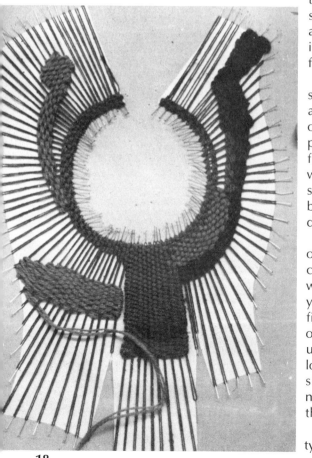

6. A pin-loom weaving in progress shows how the pin is inserted, as flat as possible; it should not protrude on the reverse side of the cardboard.

The warp is the base for a woven fabric; it is a framework made up of the threads which usually run lengthwise in loom weaving. In shaped weaving, the warp also is the base, but the threads may run in any direction.

There are many possibilities to choose from for the thread of your warp. Your decision will depend upon how you plan to use the finished product. The main things you should consider in choosing warp threads are adequate strength and very little stretch. Cotton rug warp is one of the best materials and for most tapestry weaving (where the warp is covered), you can use a neutral color of this material. However, if you plan for the warp to show, you must treat the color of the warp as an important element of the design, and base your color choice on that premise. Perle cotton (No. 5) and heavy crochet thread or other available strong yarns are also suitable warp materials.

The kind of pins you use is also important. Straight pins and round-headed ones are the best choices. Map tacks or glass-headed pins also work well, allowing the warp to slide over easily as it is being placed in position. Avoid T-pins, since the weaving threads may catch and tangle in them.

To prepare the warp, first place a pin at one edge or corner of your design. Tie the warp thread to the first pin, using an open slip knot. Then place the next pin across from the first, laying the pins as flat as possible and pointing toward each other. (See Figures 6 and 7.) It is wiser to put the pins in place as the warp is wrapped around them rather than to put all the pins in place at once. This procedure will prevent catching and tangling the threads in the pins as you prepare the warp. Pins should be placed 3/16- or 1/4-inch apart, depending upon the weight of yarn you are using for the weaving.

Place the warp securely around each pin, back and forth, from one side to the other, until you reach the end. Tie the end of the thread around the last pin with a slip knot, in the same way as you began. Now that the warp has been formed, you are ready to experience the pleasure of weaving.

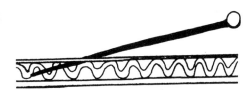

7. As in Figure 6, this drawing shows the position of the pin, as flat as possible, and not going through the cardboard to the other side.

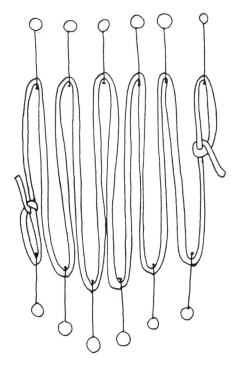

8. The beginning and end of the warp attached to pins is shown. Note that the pins face each other; this prevents the warp threads from slipping off.

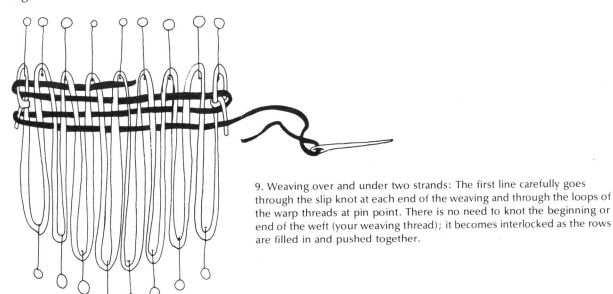

9. Weaving over and under two strands: The first line carefully goes through the slip knot at each end of the weaving and through the loops of the warp threads at pin point. There is no need to knot the beginning or end of the weft (your weaving thread); it becomes interlocked as the rows are filled in and pushed together.

10. The warping for an irregularly shaped form shows how you can set up the warp to go in two different directions. The entire form will be held together by undulating weft threads that will connect both sections of warp. The glass-headed pins used here work well in a pin loom.

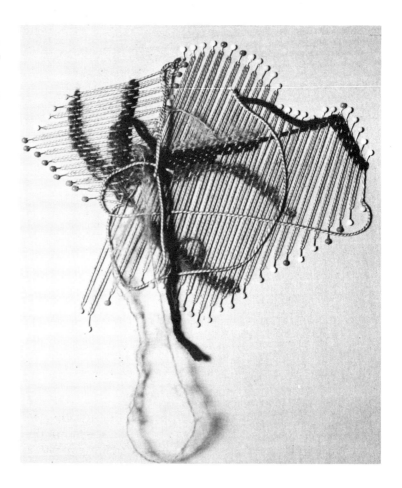

11. The warp for a slip-over neckpiece is finished. Note that the radiating pattern is irregular, the distance between the pins gradually decreasing toward the back of the piece. (Student example from the University of Washington.)

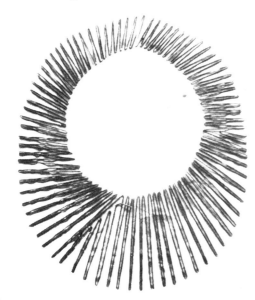

You may begin anywhere in the warp. If you start at the outside edges, however, work from the middle toward the end of a row to avoid leaving a rattail end of thread hanging at the side. (Figure 9.) The edges adjacent to the pins should be secured at the beginning by carefully weaving over and under each thread for two rows; this guarantees that the weaving edge will retain the shape the pins have delineated. The double warp thread at pin-point will not slip back into the weaving when the pins are removed if the edge has been protected as suggested by weaving over one thread and under the second at each pin-point. Remember that you should pull the beginning weaving thread through the slip knot at the edge of the warp.

The design is filled as you pick alternating threads with your needle and lay in a row or section following the planned design. Proceeding over two and under one warp thread creates a variation from the one-over-and-under scheme and fills in areas more rapidly. On the next row, the weaving should alternate — beginning with under-one-and-over-two threads if your first row started with over-two

— so that the weft threads are interlocked. As mentioned, you can start to weave anywhere on the loom. Then, you fill in areas around already-woven patterns with other colors, weights and textures of yarn. When you reach the end of a thread, simply remove the needle and overlap the end of another thread in the warp threads. You don't have to knot the new thread to the end of the other; it will stay in securely and firmly if it overlaps the end of the preceding thread.

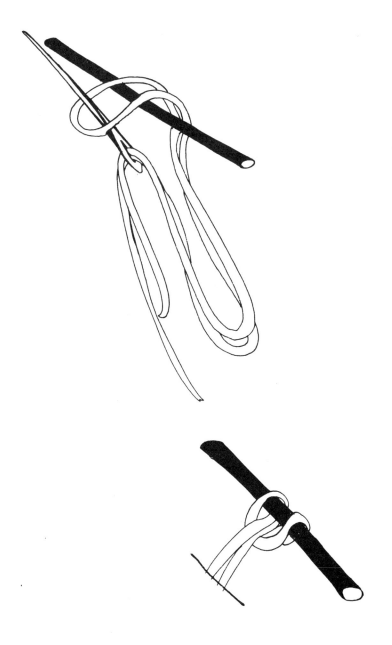

12. Double thread can be added at any time in the weaving without loose threads or thread ends showing. Simply hang the loop end of your double thread over a warp in the spot where you wish to start and then pull the double working thread through the loop.

Pin-Loom Weaving Step by Step In order to do a pin-loom weaving, first the shape is drawn on the board. (Figure 13.) You can also place a paper cutout against the board.

When you begin to warp, put the pins in place as you proceed. (Figure 14.) This simplifies the winding of the warp threads around the pins since they might otherwise catch on the pinheads while you do the warping.

Weave carefully over and under the warp at both outside edges to secure the weaving, as shown in Figure 15.

The weaving of the pattern is shown in Figure 16. You can start at any place in the loom and fill in an entire area in one color or texture before you continue on to other areas. Since you are weaving with a needle rather than a cumbersome shuttle, you can work in and out in any area, and not necessarily in straight lines.

The completed form is a collar (Figure 17, p. 24) which is ready to wear as soon as you add a hook and eye or other closure to it. It will come off the loom just as it appears on the loom and will hold together in one piece once the pins are removed. Note that all outside edges are "selvages" (the common weaving term for the edge of woven fabrics finished in such a way as to prevent raveling).

Removing a completed form from the loom is done simply by removing the pins. If you have carefully gone over and under each thread at the ends of the loom, there will be no problem. The form will hold together.

One of the many things you will discover from your first experiment in cardboard weaving is that the tension of your needle weaving is important, just as when weaving with a shuttle. You have to avoid pulling the weft too tightly as you weave to keep it from losing its shape. You will also discover that you need to push the rows together as you proceed in order to create the filled-in form. This operation is called "beating" in the weaver's vocabulary. Your product, after you are done, is a mini-tapestry which may be used in many ways, such as for patches or pockets, or other garment decorations.

Next, try another example with a different shape — perhaps a triangle, a circle or an oval — to see what different considerations come into play. In this second project, go further with texturing by trying different weaving methods — looping, knotting, using specific stitches and other techniques.

Having gotten this far, you should now plan a shaped weaving somewhat larger in scale or of greater detail. Your ambition should be tempered with caution, however. Planning a large object is fine if you are realistic about the time you have available to complete it. Otherwise, it might be safer to have modest goals at the beginning. A collar, pocket, inset, cuff, belt, necklace or any other small-sized accessory are all good first projects. But first you can also try doing samplers on looms other than the pin loom so that you can find out which loom is most suitable to the way you work.

13

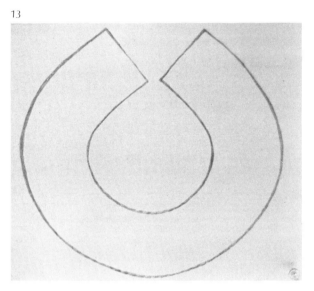

14

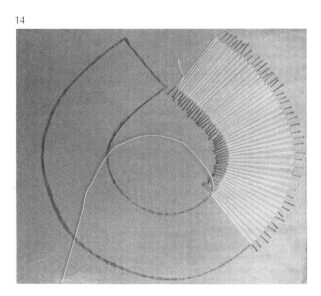

15

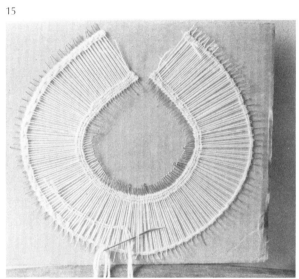

16

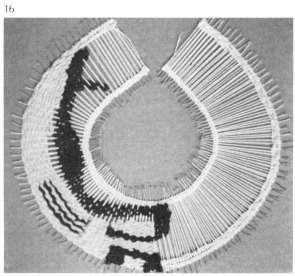

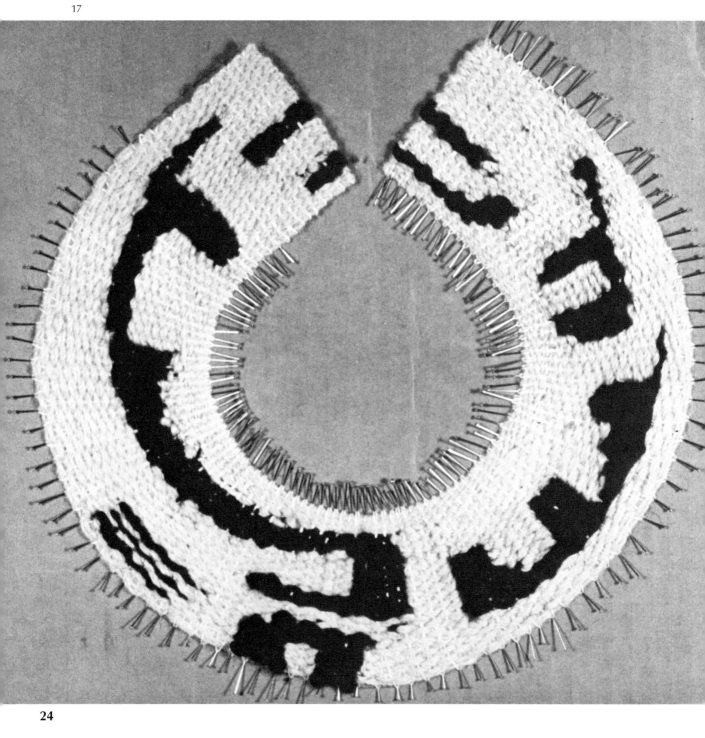

The Notched Loom Using thin and flexible cardboard, tagboard, shirt boards or chipboard (corrugated cardboard is not as suitable for this type of loom), cut a silhouette or outline shape a little larger than the proposed size of the object, about ⅛-inch all around, allowing for shrinkage of the object as it is removed when completed. Add an extra ¼ inch of space to the edges where notches will be cut. You prepare the loom by cutting notches where you wish to attach the warp threads. If your loom shape is a circle, notches should be cut all around.

Start the warp by slip-knotting one end of thread and placing it in the first notch at one corner; stretch the warp across to an opposite notch, looping the thread around the edge of the board, and proceed back in the next notch, then back and forth across the face of the cardboard until all the notches have been used. Do not put warp threads around the reverse as well as the front sides unless they are arranged in some convenient manner to allow you to slip the weaving off the loom. End the warp with a slip knot, and tape down the extending end of thread on the back of the board, or else tie the end and the beginning of the warp thread together on the back. The weaving is done in and out, over and under, back and forth, just as you did on the pin loom. When you are finished, bend the cardboard slightly in order to slip the entire woven form off the loom. This loom may be reused.

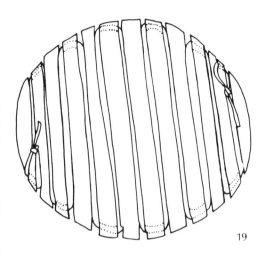

19

18, 19 and 20. The drawings on this page are of simple notched loom shapes. Warp threads are placed on the surface of the loom, passing behind it only between notches. In Figure 19, above, the dots indicate the position of the warp thread on the reverse side of the loom.

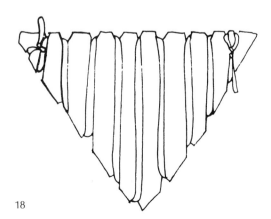

18

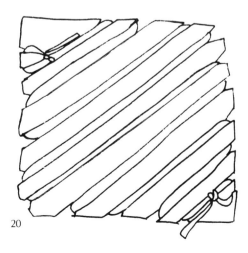

20

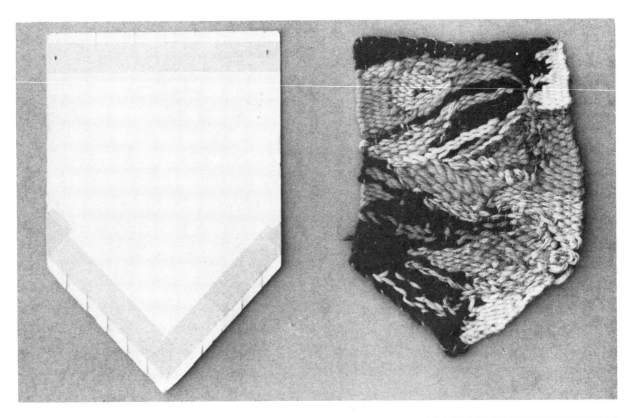

21. A slit-edge loom is shown and next to it the finished example after it was removed. Note the apparent shrinkage in the finished piece; this is typical in weaving but comes as a suprise to the novice when he removes his first weaving from the loom.

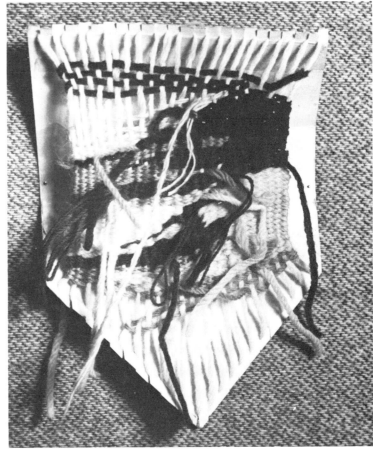

22. As tension increases the loom may begin to bow, but if the cardboard is flexible, this is no problem. Actually it becomes an advantage since the space between the weaving and the loom makes for easier execution of the weaving process.

The Slit-Edge Loom Identical in principle but different in the nature of the cuts at the edge is the slit-edge loom. Tagboard and other strong thin board are good to use for a slit-edge loom. Cut the cardboard on all sides in the shape of the object you are making. The cardboard should be ¼-inch longer at each end that will be slit than the final size of the object. Cut in approximately ¼-inch from the edges wherever you wish warp threads to be attached. The slits should be of uniform length and spaced evenly apart, ¼-inch or less between each slit. For straightness and strength, place a strip of masking tape at the inner edge of the slits on both the front and the back of the loom. Then attach the warp as in the notched cardboard loom. The completed form may be slipped off this loom very easily, as with the notched loom.

Stitch-Edge Looms Draw the desired shape of your form on thin, flexible cardboard, leaving at least one inch of cardboard around the outline. Then, using No. 5 Perle cotton and a sharp, pointed needle, sew a running stitch around the outline until you return to the beginning point. Continue once again around the form in the same direction, filling in the alternating spaces, and ending where you began. Tie the end and the beginning of the thread into a knot. The stitch outline will be the attaching device for your warp threads; it will perform the same function as the pins in the pin loom.

For the warping, thread suitable yarn into a needle and begin at a corner on the outline by attaching the warp thread to the outline stitching with a loose slip knot. Then attach the warp onto a point of the outline thread opposite where you began. Continue warping as in the pin loom method, bringing the warp around under each stitch and being sure to attach the warps around the stitch holes periodically in order to hold the threads in place. The weaving is done just as in the other methods.

To remove the weaving from the cardboard, cut the outline thread *on the back*. When this outline thread has been removed, the woven form will be released from its outline loom.

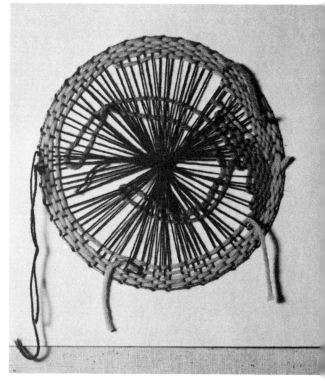

23. This example in progress of a circular form with overlapping warp threads will have open areas including the center, where overlapping itself creates a radial design.

How to Proceed with Your Stitch-Loom Weaving Stitching back and forth on tagboard (or other thin flexible cardboard) creates the outline for the shaped form. (Figure 24.)

The stitch loom is warped by tying the warp onto the stitch edge, then laying it in back and forth, looming it around the outline thread, as in Figure 25.

Since the stitched thread outline for the loom is duplicated in mirror image on the back of the cardboard, two similar shaped forms can be woven before the outline threads are cut to release the weavings from the loom. The illustrations in Figures 26 and 27 are two forms from the two sides of the same stitch loom.

24

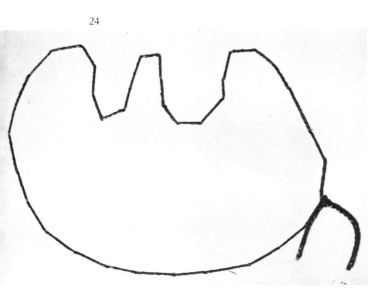

26

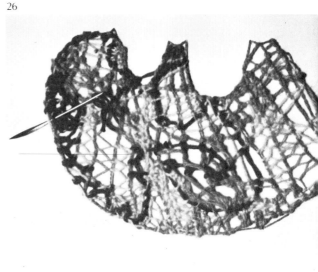

25

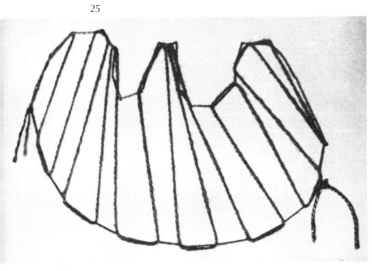

27

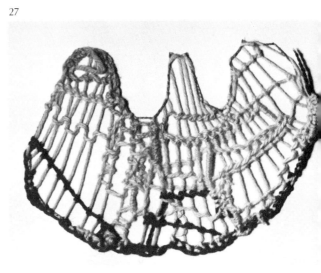

The Stitch-Edge Loom: Needle-Lace Technique Weaving on this type of loom is done in the same way as on the pin loom. The example in Figure 28 shows the open weave treatment that is characteristic of a needle lace technique. The weft threads are securely knotted into place or merely twisted around the warp. You can use a wide variety of combinations of weave in this open way of working. The end product may be used as a decorative element added to a garment.

28. This finished needle-lace shape will be applied to a garment as open net-work decoration. Note the wide variety of detached stitches incorporated in this one example.

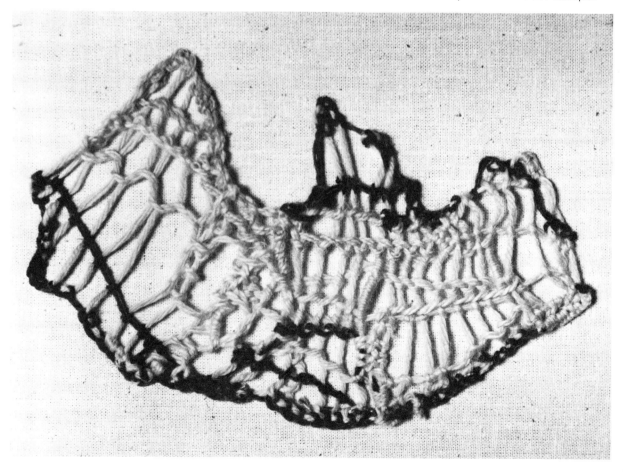

Machine-Stitched Outline A sewing machine may be used to advantage in the beginning stages of creating the stitch-edge loom. Set the machine at the largest stitch (6 to the inch), and use the unthreaded needle as a spacer. After the holes have been evenly punched in, you can enlarge them with a pointed needle or an awl, and you can use every second or third hole if larger distances between are called for. The prepunched holes will facilitate the stitching of the outline so that you won't tear or fold the thin cardboard during this step of preparing the loom.

A more direct method is to actually stitch the outline by machine, using the heaviest machine thread with loose tension. The thread outline will be strong enough to hold a warp of No. 5 Perle cotton or carpet warp yarn. Your weaving can include any techniques you may already have mastered such as tabby, twill weave, interlocked tapestry, slit tapestry, soumak, giordes knot, or rya weaving. Remove the finished form by carefully cutting and removing the sewing machine stitching. Cut the outline thread *on the back* of the loom to avoid the danger of cutting any warp threads.

29. Evenly spaced machine-stitched thread is the outline to which the warp thread is attached. First threaded into a needle, the warp must be slipped through the loose tension of the machine thread.

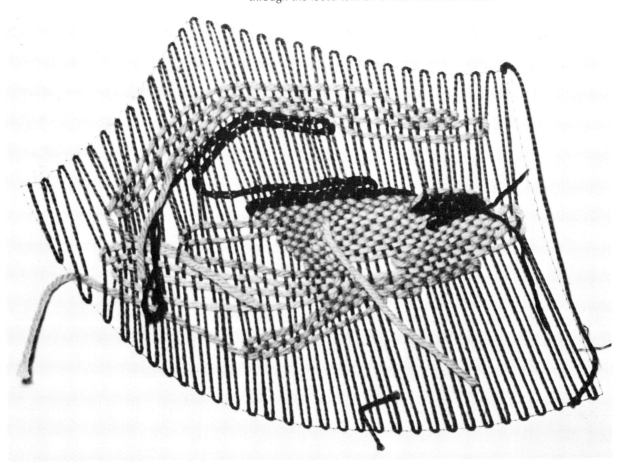

Spoke Weaving

Round forms are easily woven on a bicycle wheel frame or any other hoop that has evenly spaced holes. The warp is attached to the frame through the holes and overlaps in the center as it crosses. The weaving is begun at the center and continues until the desired size of the piece is reached. You can cut off a small form from the middle of the frame, leaving a good bit of the warp threads attached to it which can then be used to bind the form to a background. When wooden or plastic hoops are used, the warp threads can be tied or wrapped around the hoop and stretched across. To control the spacing, spread beads of white glue onto the hoop at the points where you intend the warps to remain; otherwise, there may be some slipping.

The same methods on small ring forms, such as brass drapery rings, can be used to create miniature pieces for use as jewelry or decoration on other weaving. (See the jewelry section of this book for examples of other wire frameworks, pp. 81–89).

30. The warp threads are attached to holes in a bicycle wheel rim and are tied.

31. Note the length of warps that remain unfilled. There must be enough warp thread left to cut and weave back into the piece unless you want the object to remain on the rim. After the warp threads have been removed from the rim, thread them on a needle and stitch them back into the woven area.

32. A detail of the weaving shows the overlapping warp threads at the center.

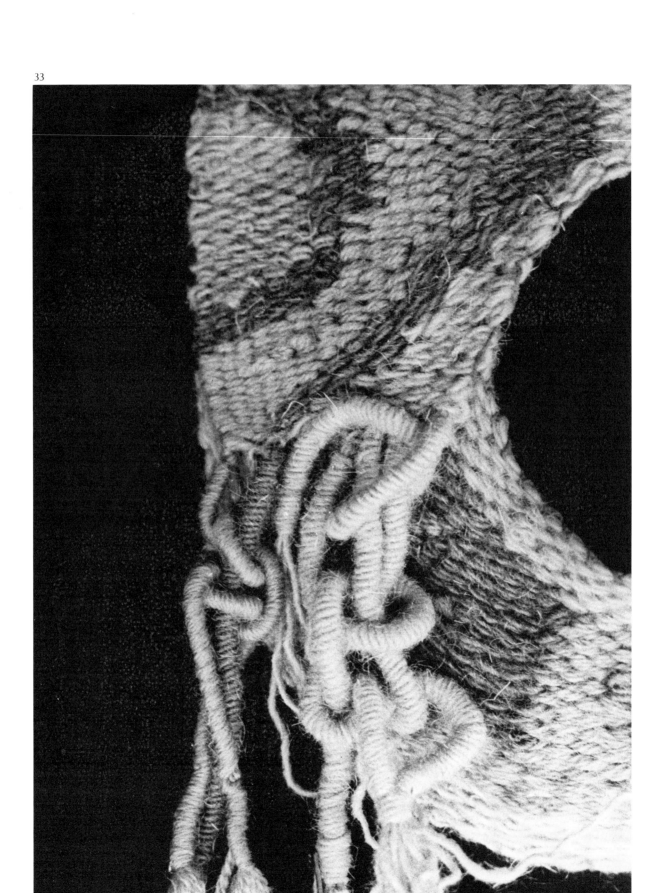

No-Loom Techniques

Wrapping One of the most effective techniques for adding decoration, or for varying and assembling shaped weavings, is wrapping, which is simply achieved through a variety of methods of winding yarn around cords, groups of threads, warps or dangling fringe. Usually, the yarn is tied around its own end to secure it.

The working yarn should be tied around a looped end of itself against the cord it is covering. Continue wrapping until the desired wrapped effect or length is achieved. The remaining yarn should then be fastened in by pulling it into the wrapped form with a needle. The protruding end can be cut.

If the cord you are wrapping is loose at at least one end, the simple method to use is to place the wrapping yarn ends opposite each other and extending beyond the beginning and end of the cord to be wrapped. Hold both ends and the cord securely in one hand and wrap with the other. Start at the open end or bottom of the cord. Wrap tightly and continue up the cord as you work. When you reach the end, work the remaining thread into the wrapping by pulling the exposed end at the bottom (or beginning) of the cord. If you pull it tightly, the wrapping will be neat and secure, and the end will be hidden inside the work. The extra yarn can be cut off. (See Wrapping Method 2, Figure 35.)

Wrapping Method 1   Start wrapping around the core thread and around one end of the thread used for wrapping. When you reach the desired length, thread the wrapping thread into a needle and stitch it into the wrapping, back toward the starting end. Clip the protruding thread for a neat wrap. (Figure 34.)

Wrapping Method 2   Place the wrapping thread in a loop over the core, with ends A and B facing opposite directions. Hold both the core and wrap thread securely in one hand and wrap with the other, starting near end A and wrapping toward end B. The wrapping can cover end B. When you have reached the desired length of wrapped cord (or when the loop gets too short to continue), draw the remaining loop securely into the wrapping by pulling the exposed end A. With the wrap tightened, clip off any remainder of it at end A (and at B also if that end has not been covered in the wrapping). To use this method, the core must be free at end A. (Figure 35.)

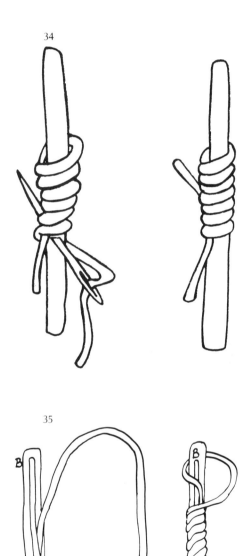

34

35

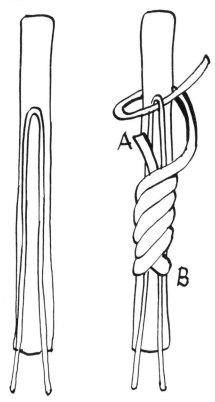

Wrapping Method 3 Lay an extra hairpin-looped thread onto the core, leaving the ends opposite the loop extended beyond the beginning of the intended wrapping. Place the end of wrapping yarn near the loop and start wrapping at the bottom (B) (or loose-ends point of the hairpin) and work up toward the loop (A). When you reach the loop, slip the working thread into it; (make sure you have allowed sufficient length to pull the thread end back through the wrap). The loop acts as the eye of a needle: After threading it, pull it through the wrapping until it emerges at the bottom or beginning end. Remove the hairpin and trim off the protruding end of the wrap thread. (Figure 36.)

Wrapping Method 4 Self-wrapping, or warp wrapping, is used to cover exposed warp threads in the middle of the weaving, or to add decorative threads on the surface of the piece. For this method, the needle remains threaded with the wrapping thread throughout.

Wrapping across or over woven areas can add a decorative effect to the weaving. This is done by stitching back and forth, attaching ends to the same points to establish a core to wrap around. The wrapping can start with the same thread that is used for the core and then terminate at the opposite end when the core is adequately covered. Simply stitch the thread into the weaving.

This method can also be used for covering exposed warp

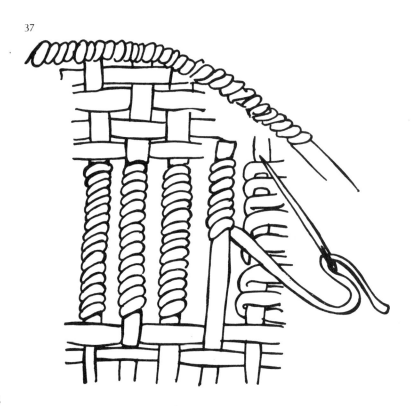

threads in the middle of the weaving. To cover open areas of warp, attach the wrapping thread to the adjacent woven area, stitching it in. After securely wrapping it around the warp (or warps), attach the remaining wrapping thread to the opposite woven section, stitching it back and forth so that it is interlocked. (Figure 37.)

Wrapping Method 5 Place one end of the wrapping thread in a loop (C) against the core. Start wrapping with the working end of the wrapping thread near the bottom, leaving loose end A exposed. Wrap up toward the loop until the desired length is reached. Slip the working end of the thread (B) through the loop (C). Then pull end A until the loop and the working end *B* are securely hidden under the wrapping. For a trim and neat end, cut *A* close to the wrapped section at point *D*. (Figure 38.)

Coiling: A Related Technique Coiling is done by loosely looping or twisting thread around itself. After twisting the thread several times, pull both ends. With this technique you will get a beaded section similar to the results of self-wrapping (Figure 39).

Other related techniques in macramé can also be used effectively. For example, square knotting works well in covering a center core.

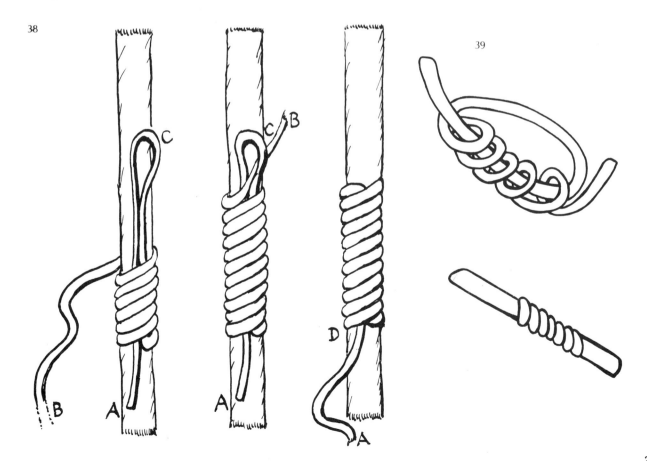

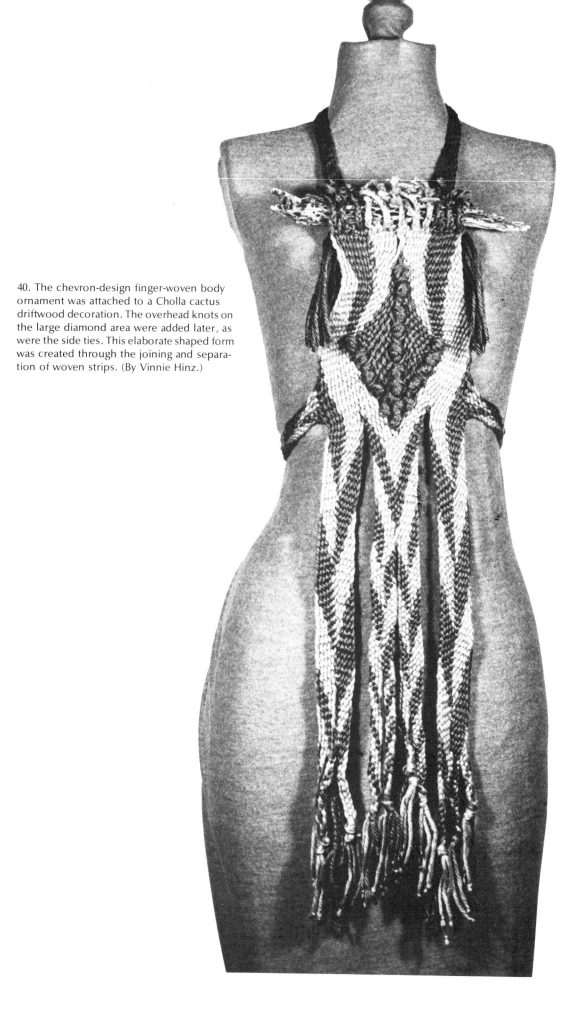

40. The chevron-design finger-woven body ornament was attached to a Cholla cactus driftwood decoration. The overhead knots on the large diamond area were added later, as were the side ties. This elaborate shaped form was created through the joining and separation of woven strips. (By Vinnie Hinz.)

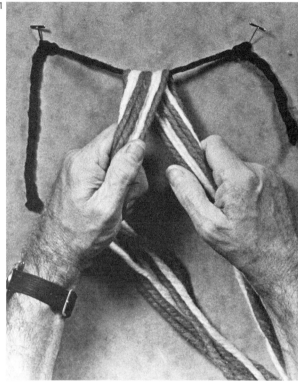

41

Finger Weaving Finger weaving is a convenient term for a variety of simple loomless and tool-less techniques which lend themselves well to making narrow forms that fit conveniently into the hands. However, it is not difficult to extend the technique and make rather complicated and broad objects. To some, finger weaving is braiding or plaiting, the principles of which it employs; but it also may be done as true weaving with separate, rather than self-warps.

To prepare for your work, you need some simple device as a working surface. A cord to tie your work to — as is done in many knotting and netting techniques — is one method. You can pin the cord to a heavy cardboard surface or nail it to a block of wood. Some people prefer to use Bull Clips or clamps; and a clipboard works very well too.

Choose your materials wisely. Use heavy (bulky) yarns for your first exercises, such as knitting or rug yarns, so that you may work quickly, and leave finer details for later projects. Select two or more colors approximately three times the length of the finished article. You need nothing more — your fingers are your tools.

Step-by-Step Finger Weaving from One Side 1. Start by pinning the holding cord to the working surface (or by clamping the yarn with a heavy clip). Fold the threads in half over the holding cord. This creates top and bottom layers of threads which are lined up in a pattern of your own choosing. Now you are ready for the actual finger weaving (Figure 41).

2. Separate and align the threads by holding them tightly in your left hand with your index finger between the two layers. The space the finger now occupies is called the shed. (Figure 42.)

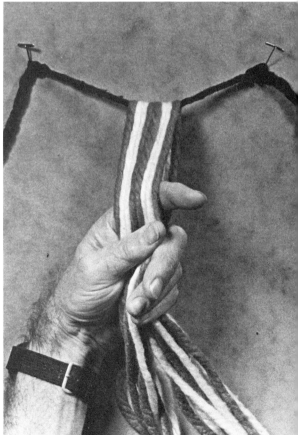

42

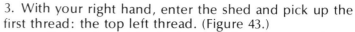

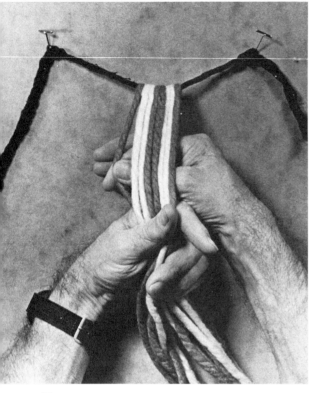

43

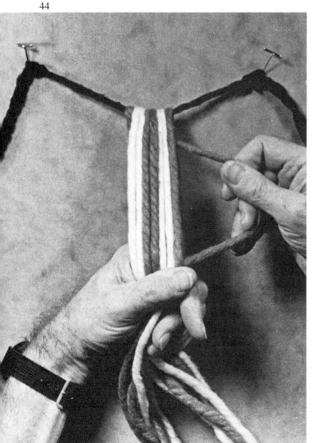

44

3. With your right hand, enter the shed and pick up the first thread: the top left thread. (Figure 43.)

4. Pull the thread back through the shed and hold it tightly in your right hand between the index finger and the middle finger. (Figure 44.)

5. This thread has now moved from the upper left to the lower right, and for this row of weaving it has become the weft. This is the pattern that every thread will follow in this method of finger weaving. (Figure 45.)

6. Now, to change the shed, pick up the first right lower thread with your thumb and index finger and leave it on the index finger. (Figure 46.)

7. Pick up the next thread, which is an upper one, with your index and middle fingers, and hold it tightly between the index finger and middle finger. (Figure 47.)

8. Continue adding alternating threads onto the index and middle fingers of the right hand until you reach the left edge of the row, having thus transferred all threads to the right hand. Remember to hold all the threads at all times, since tension is as important in this form of weaving as in all the others and releasing the threads at any time creates irregularity of tension. For correct and uniform weaving, equal tension of the warp threads is essential; this is achieved by holding all the threads firmly as you work. (Figure 48.)

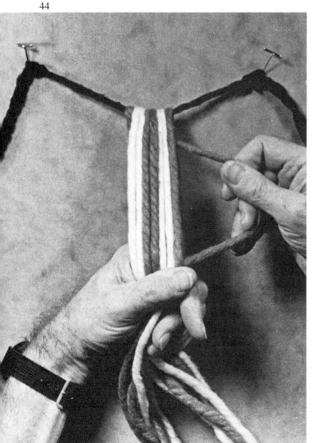

44

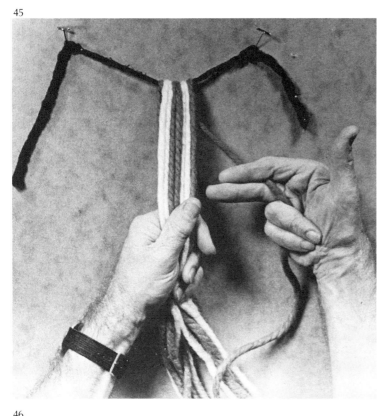

45

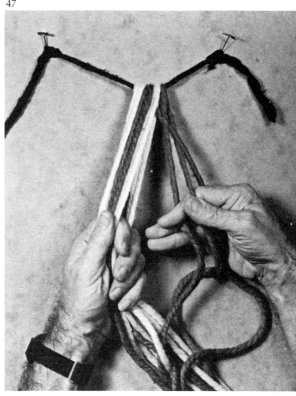

47

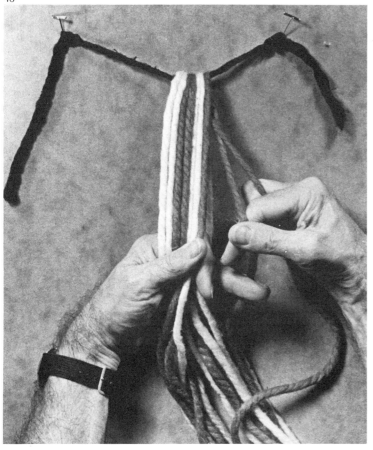

46

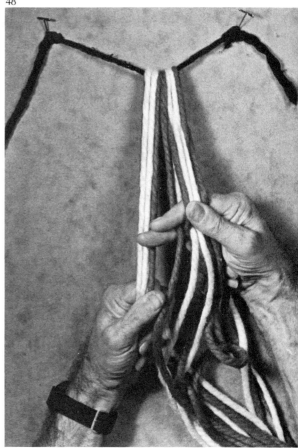

48

49

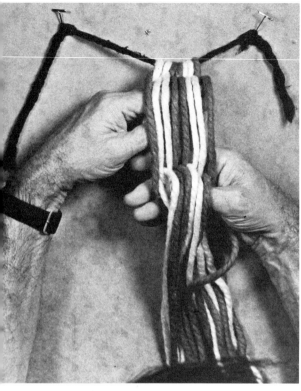

51

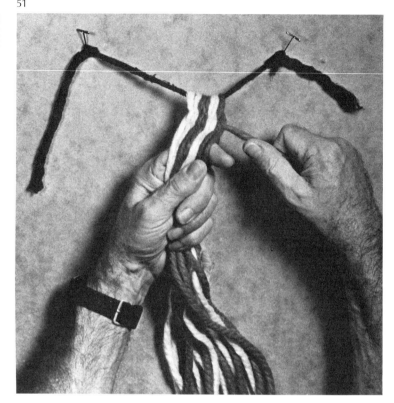

50

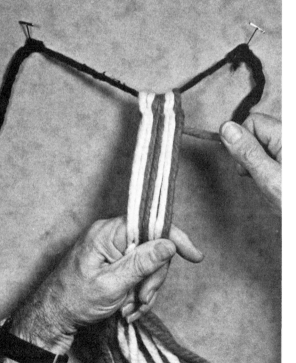

52

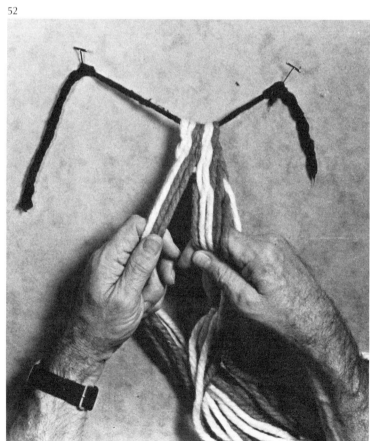

40

9. To tighten a woven row, push your left index finger up against what you have woven ("beating"). As you do this, transfer all the threads in proper order to your left hand, which grasps them as soon as the beating (or pushing up) is done. (Figure 49.)

10. While your right hand is free, pull the last woven thread to the right so that it is hidden by the warp. By doing this, you also establish and control the evenness of the width of the object you are weaving. After tightening, drop the pulled thread so that it becomes the last right lower thread. (Figure 50.)

11. With your left hand holding the work, and the index finger opening the shed, the weaving is ready for a continuation of the entire process just described. (Figure 51.)

12. Keep weaving until you have reached the desired length of the object. (Figure 52.)

13. As you continue weaving, note that the pattern becomes a diagonal design, since all the weaving is from one side. (Figure 53.)

14. Once you have completed a simple straight example, you are ready to experiment with shaping your finger weaving. This may be accomplished by variation in tension as you curve the form. (Figure 54.)

53

54
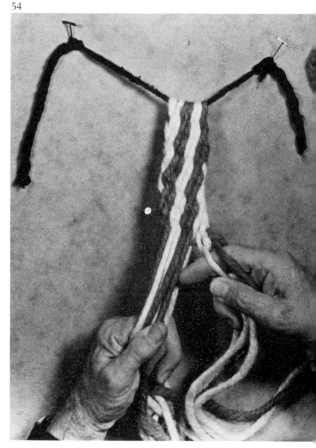

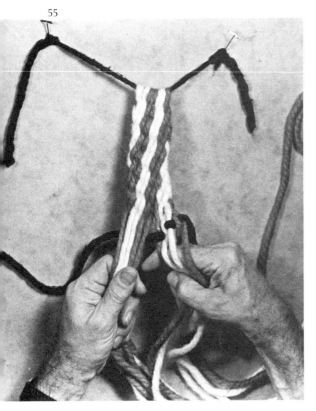

55

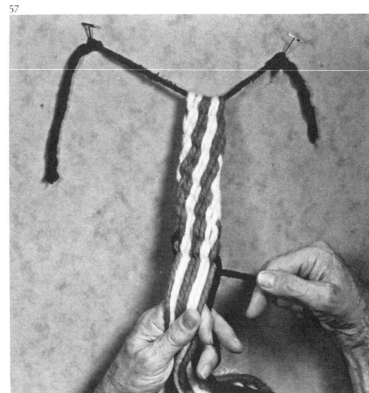

57

56

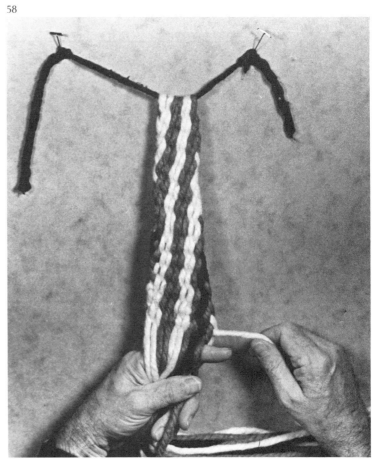

58

15. The object is gradually widened by progressively adding threads to extend its width. (Figure 55.) The threads are laid into the open shed and then the process previously described is continued; just be careful to incorporate each new thread at both edges of the weaving, as follows.

16. Change the shed and hold the right side of the new thread tightly in your right hand. Carefully pull the thread on the left side to create proper tension. The free thread on the left is ready to be pulled through the shed with your right forefinger. (Figure 56.)

17. The left hand grasps the work by inserting the forefinger in the shed as the right forefinger pulls the new thread through. (Figure 57.)

18. As threads are added, the pattern continues to be a diagonal stripe as long as the weaving is done from the same side. The example illustrated is woven from left to right. (Figure 58.)

With finger weaving, the variety of patterns you can make depends on how you arrange the threads. (Figure 59.) In Figure 60, the grouping of the threads creates a chevron pattern. Here the weaving was done from the middle to each side.

In Figure 61, a vertical stripe pattern resulted from the alignment of alternating colors and weaving with an extra strand. The weft thread color shows only at the edges. Finger weaving is usually only thought of as warp-design weaving.

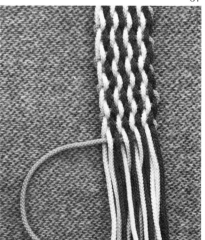

The horizontal pattern in Figure 62 resulted from an arrangement of the threads in which all the threads of one color were placed on top of all the threads of another color and the weaving was done with a separate weft, which is optional. The weft may be any color or weight. Widening of the piece is shown at the right of the figure.

The front of the finger-woven bag in Figure 63 has braided fringe and beads. The weaving strands were attached to a rounded wooden handle before the weaving began, and the weaving was done from the center to both sides in tones of yellow and brown. The bag, which was created by Jonda Friel, is backed with fabric in related colors. (See also C-10 in the color section.)

63

62

Part II: Examples

Patches

Unusual shapes of any kind can be made and used as patches for a variety of garments and purposes. You can combine patches in coordinated colors to decorate an outfit or ensemble and can thus achieve any effect from very formal to whimsical or humorous. Patches are good for trimming edges as well as for dynamic placement in the center of garments.

The patch decoration should be planned for the garment it is to enhance: color and texture should be considered. Patches should either harmonize or contrast with the fabric they are applied to. It is wise to avoid colorful decorative patches on garments which are patterned or highly textured and rich in themselves; the woven patch functions better as embellishment to accent a simple outfit. Its potential is great, and it may easily make the difference between an ordinary garment and one which is truly unique and distinctive. Through this simple device, you have the opportunity of truly personalizing your wardrobe.

Free-form patches can take any shape. The two shown in Figures 64 and 65 on the next page were designed as a pair and were planned as appliqués for jeans or slacks. You can weave long strips on as few as two threads simply by going over and under back and forth. (Figure 65.)

Irregular patches appliquéd to slacks personalize an outfit. (Figures 66 and 67 on page 47.) A complete ensemble gains distinction through the addition of unique ornamental patches.

A close-up detail of Figure 64.

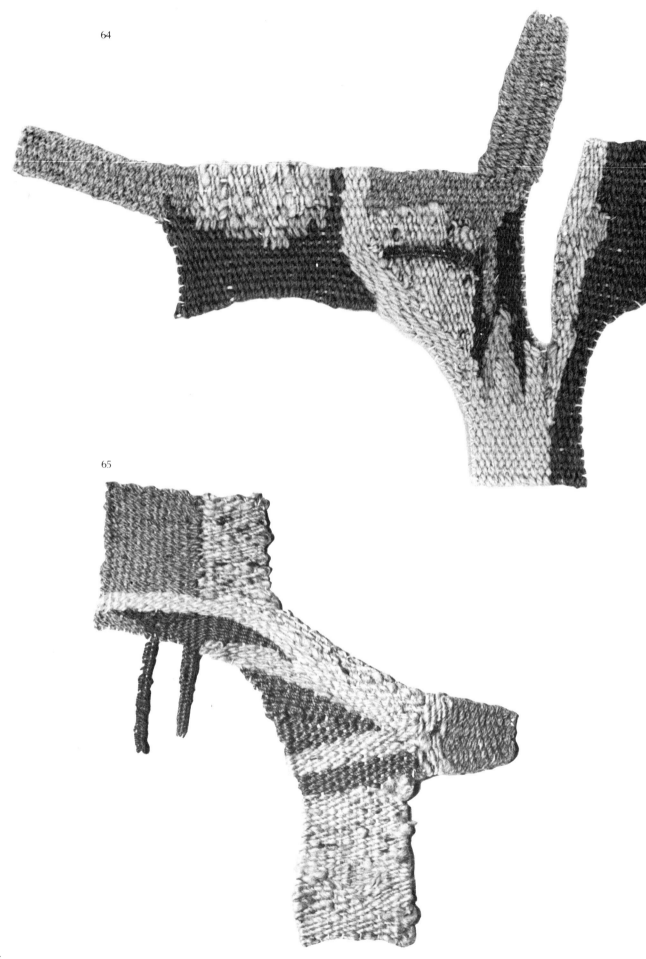

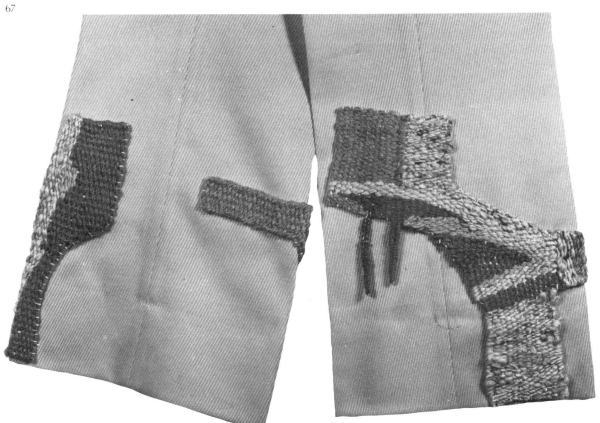

The drawings demonstrate some other possibilities for placement and shapes of patches on various garments. (Figures 68, 69, 70 and 71.)

68

70

71

69

Pockets

The woven patch can take on the form and added function of a pocket. The simple pocket shape in Figures 72 and 73 shows a pattern that was achieved with a variety of color and weave effects — alternating over one, under one; over two, back one.

In Figure 74, a deep pocket was given an additional woven strip. The strip, which is attached at its top and bottom, may be woven after you have completed the basic form. You merely stitch the four warp threads to the opposite ends of the piece, and then weave onto them.

72

74

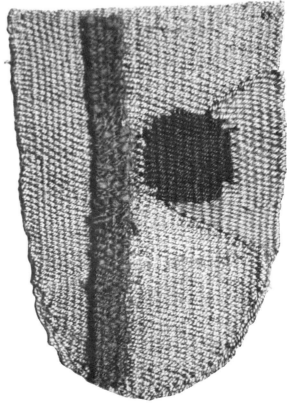

73

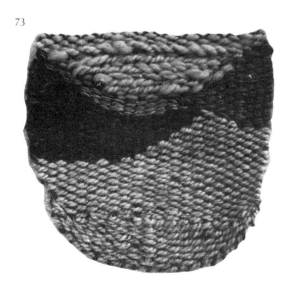

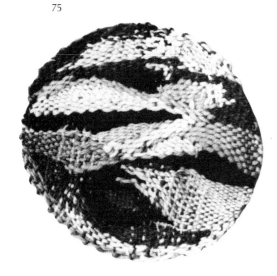

75

The two examples shown in Figure 75 were created on a stitch-edge loom. A solid circle was warped with parallel threads. The circle with the opening had an additional stitch outline — the radius providing an edge to which opposite warps were strung. When the weaving was completed, this edge became the slit or opening for a pocket.

When a woven patch pocket is made to conform to and cover an existing slacks pocket, it can look like the one in Figure 76. (See also C-13 in the color section.) Remember to make the loom slightly larger than the finished object, to allow for take-up or shrinkage when the object is removed from the loom.

76

Appliqués

Shaped patches have a wide variety of appliqué possibilities. In Figure 77 we see a caftan whose large-scale decoration is equally effective worn in the front or the back. The robe is also a unisex garment and can be worn for many different occasions. (Figure 78.) Other related garments like kimonos and ecclesiastical vestments lend themselves to shaped weaving embellishment. Dresses and capes offer limitless opportunities for this kind of treatment. Some suggestions appear on the next two pages in Figures 79 through 85.

78

77

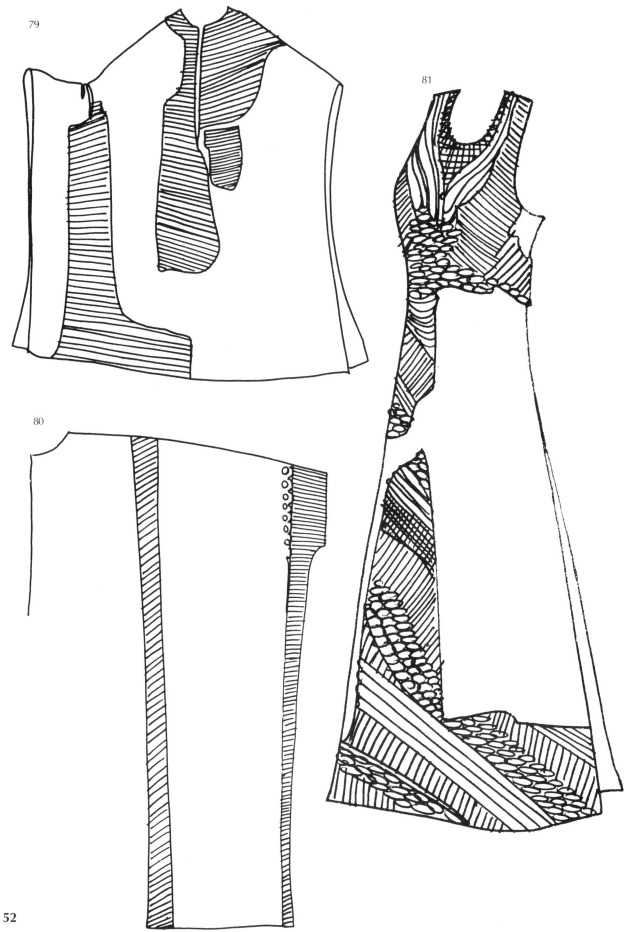

79

80

81

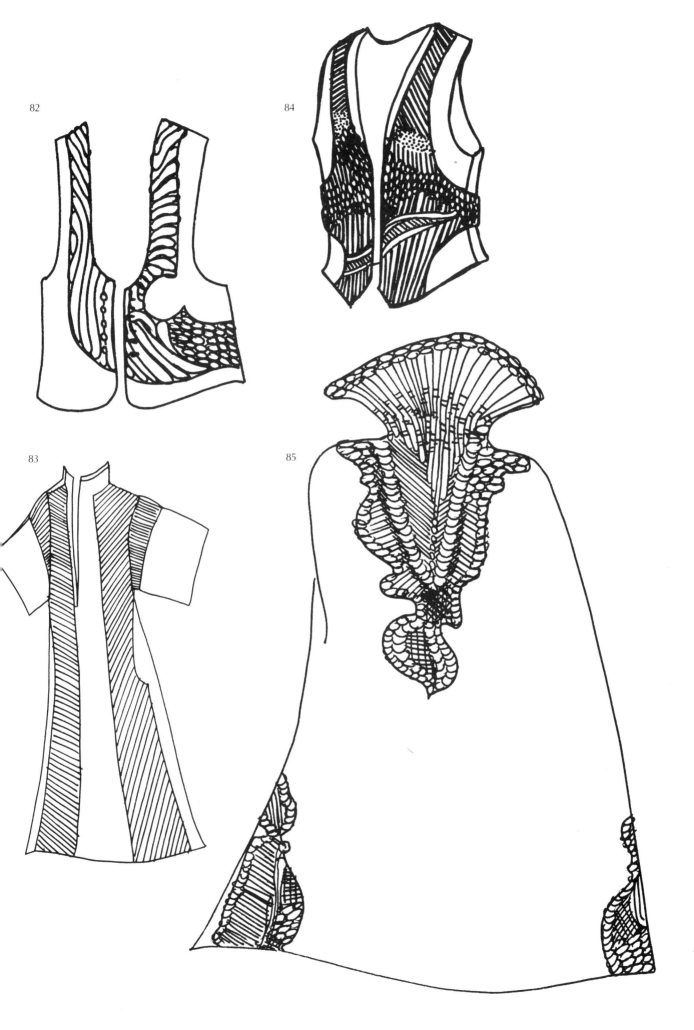

82

84

83

85

Symbols, Emblems and Insignias

The need for appliqué patches for identification of clubs and other groups is endless, and the vogue for attaching emblems to sweaters and jackets is everpresent, especially among high school and college students. The easiest method of all for creating unique and effective popular patches is needle weaving on cardboard looms.

Letters and numbers, as well as symbols like the peace symbol, patriotic signs, flags, stars, the eagle, human and animal figures and other forms may be easily made on these looms. You can include detail if you work with fine yarns, but it is wise to leave this challenge until you have become adept at the technique. No matter what you do, think of the scale of the object; the scale of the weaving material should be directly related to it. A large bold form can be quickly done with heavy or bulky yarns; a small-scale delicate arm patch should be done with fine warp and lightweight yarns, and with a fine blunt-tip needle. Thus, a delicate miniature may take as long to do as a full-scale garment.

Shaped weaving lends itself to figurative treatment as well as geometric or abstract shapes. The natural forms of flora and fauna can be rendered. However, in order to do them in the bold techniques of pin-loom weaving you must simplify their design. Animal and bird shapes, such as those shown in Figures 88, 89 and 90, have many applications, perhaps most obviously on children's garments or accessories, or as emblems for schools or teams.

86. In this bird form in progress, note the varied directions of the warp threads and how the pins are used to change warp direction.

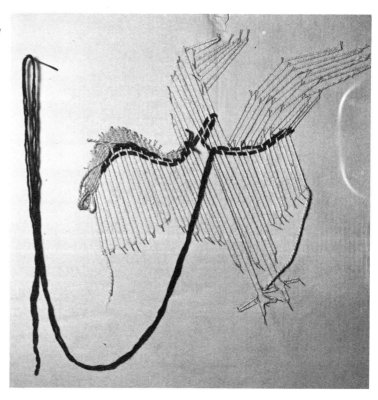

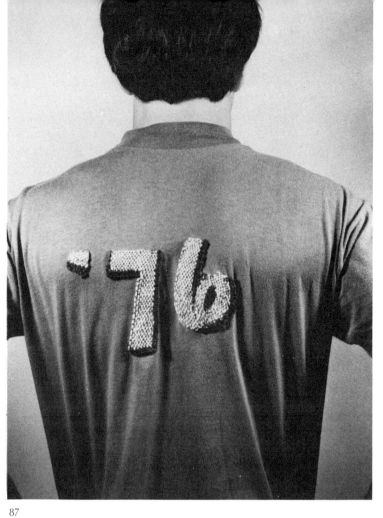

87. Numerals are simple-shaped forms to make, as are letters. The three-dimensional effect in this example was created through color variations.

87

89

88

90

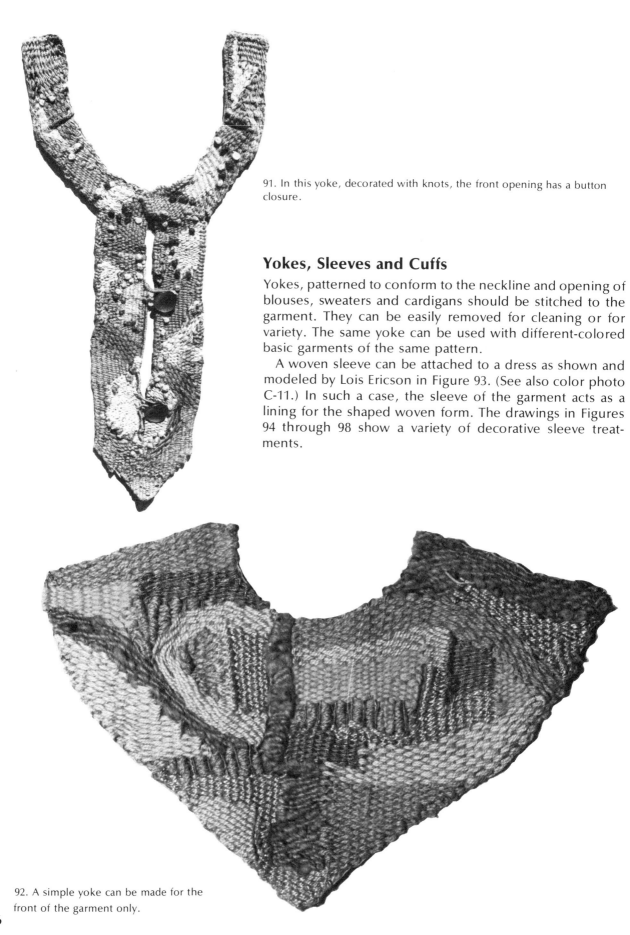

91. In this yoke, decorated with knots, the front opening has a button closure.

Yokes, Sleeves and Cuffs

Yokes, patterned to conform to the neckline and opening of blouses, sweaters and cardigans should be stitched to the garment. They can be easily removed for cleaning or for variety. The same yoke can be used with different-colored basic garments of the same pattern.

A woven sleeve can be attached to a dress as shown and modeled by Lois Ericson in Figure 93. (See also color photo C-11.) In such a case, the sleeve of the garment acts as a lining for the shaped woven form. The drawings in Figures 94 through 98 show a variety of decorative sleeve treatments.

92. A simple yoke can be made for the front of the garment only.

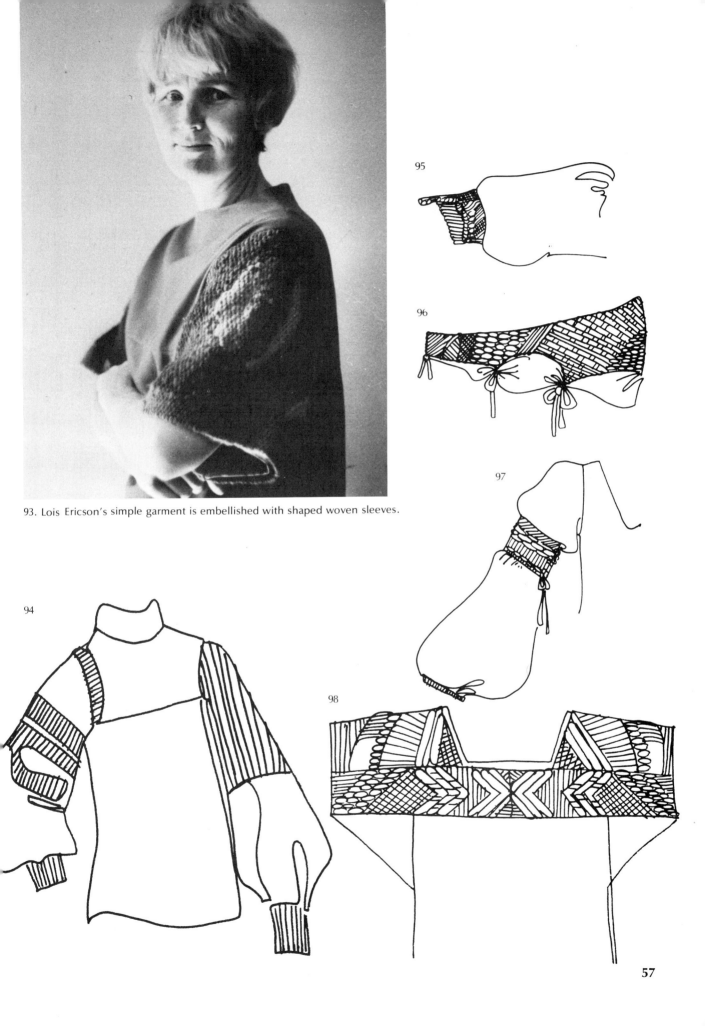

93. Lois Ericson's simple garment is embellished with shaped woven sleeves.

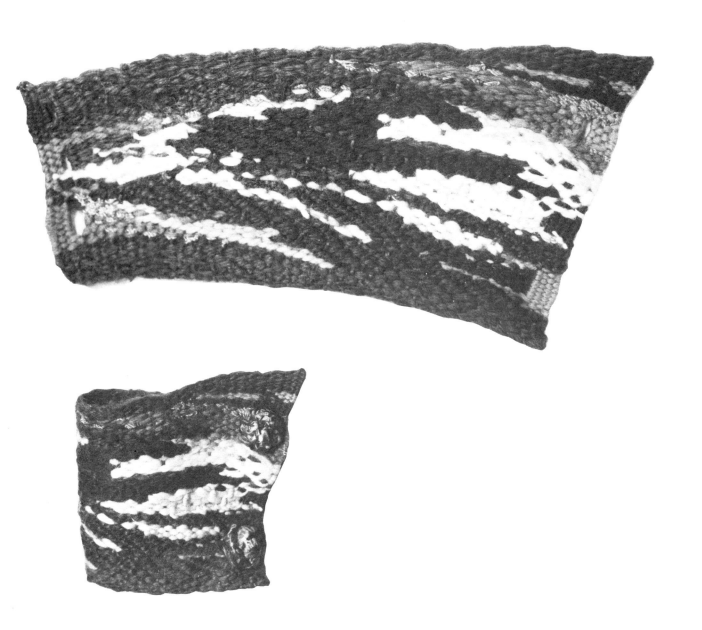

99. The cuff shape, spread out, shows the complete pattern.

The cuff shape shown in Figure 99 was woven with the slit tapestry technique at the sides where the buttons or cuff links are to be inserted. You can wear such cuffs separately or stitch them to the sleeves of garments. The buttons were cloth covered and stitched in colors that harmonize with the cuffs.

100. The cuff is buttoned with special cloth-covered buttons.

Collars and Other Neckpieces

Collars and neckpieces are other useful and decorative articles that can be needle-woven on cardboard looms.

The neckpiece shown in Figure 101 was woven with white flax, brown rayon and green wool and was accented with a pelt of assorted feathers in related colors and of iridescent texture. Note the arrangement of dark and light patterns in the piece. (See also color photo C-6.)

The elaborate pectoral shown on the next page incorporates sections of a silver necklace from Iran. Two separate woven sections were joined by open wrapped looped cords and silver pieces. The weaving has subtle gradations of color and is a simple background against which to set off the wrapped attachments and jewelry.

Beads can be attached to a piece before you start to weave. (Figure 103, p. 61.) You add them to the warp as the weaving progresses by temporarily removing the warps from one pin, slipping the bead onto the double warp thread and then replacing the loop of thread around the pin. Exactly where to place the bead is up to you. You can move it back and forth along the warp thread until you have decided.

The collar in Figure 106 (p. 61) is enhanced by the decorative use of wrapped yarns. Extra threads are added as fringe to the edge of the object and are then covered with wrapping for variety. The twisted wrappings create an effective mass at the edges where the piece is joined. Wrapping can be done around many threads which are left free at the ends to create a tassel effect.

101. (Collection of Virginia Hamill Johnson.)

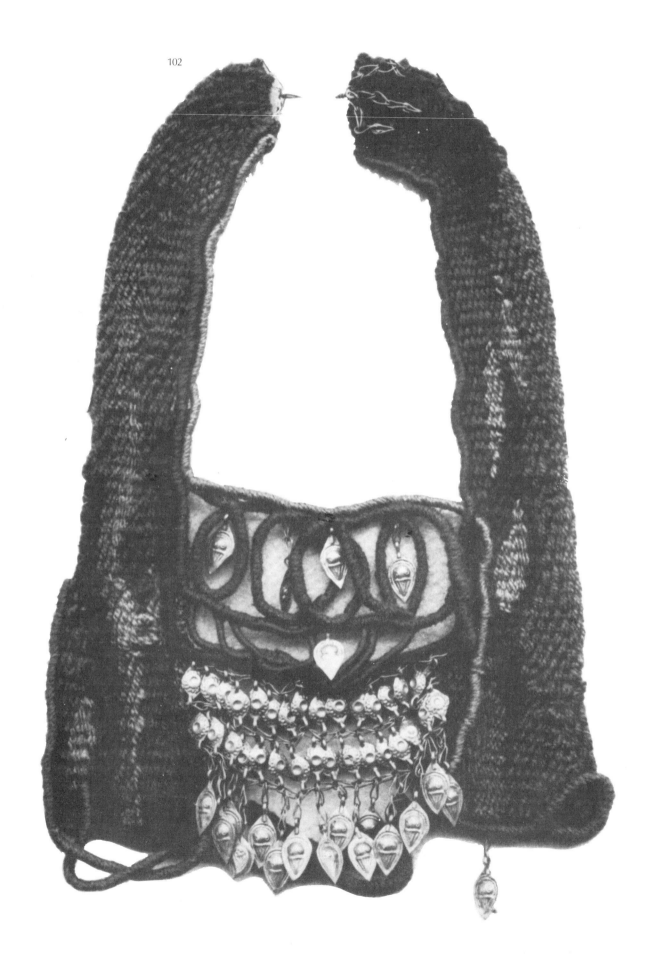

102

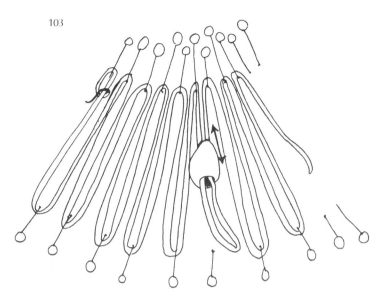

103

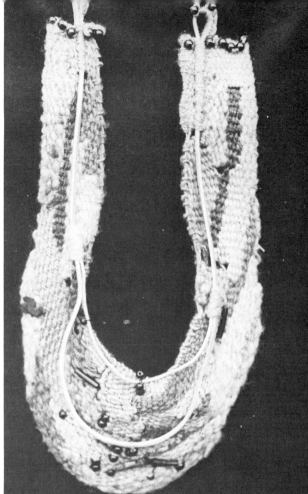

Below: 104. A close-up view of Figure 105.

Upper right: 105. To a simple collar were added wooden beads and leather thong decoration and closure.

106

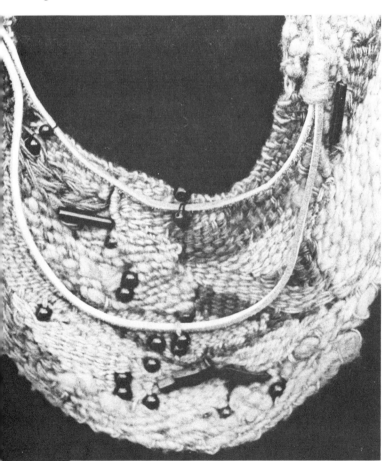

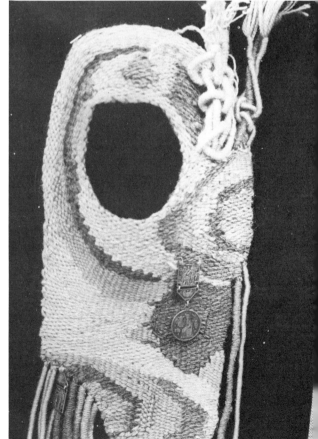

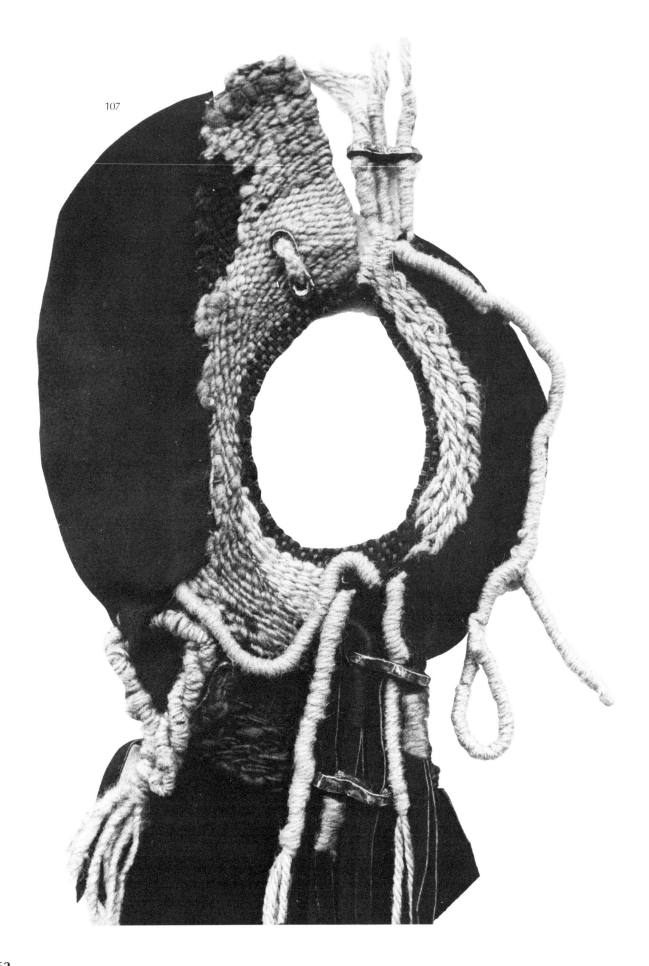

In Figure 107, you see finger weaving that has been interwoven between separate pieces of leather to form a garment. Holes were punched along the edges of the leather and weaving threads were added progressively and woven to each other as they were looped through the holes of the leather. This is an excellent method of using shaped weaving (in this case, finger-woven), to build a garment composed of sections of leather, fur or felt.

The finger-woven collar in Figure 108 was done in black and gray handspun wool and trimmed with metal chain mail and ball buttons. Wrapped threads were distributed on the face of this neckpiece and were also used extensively where the two strands overlap and join at the back.

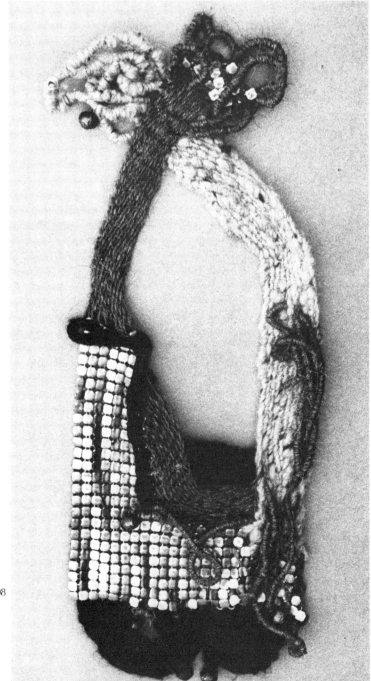

108

109. A detail of the collar in Figure 108 shows the weaving and wrapping. .

Facing page: 110. The finger-woven collar can be worn over any garment. (Made by Lois Ericson and modeled by Nik Krevitsky.)

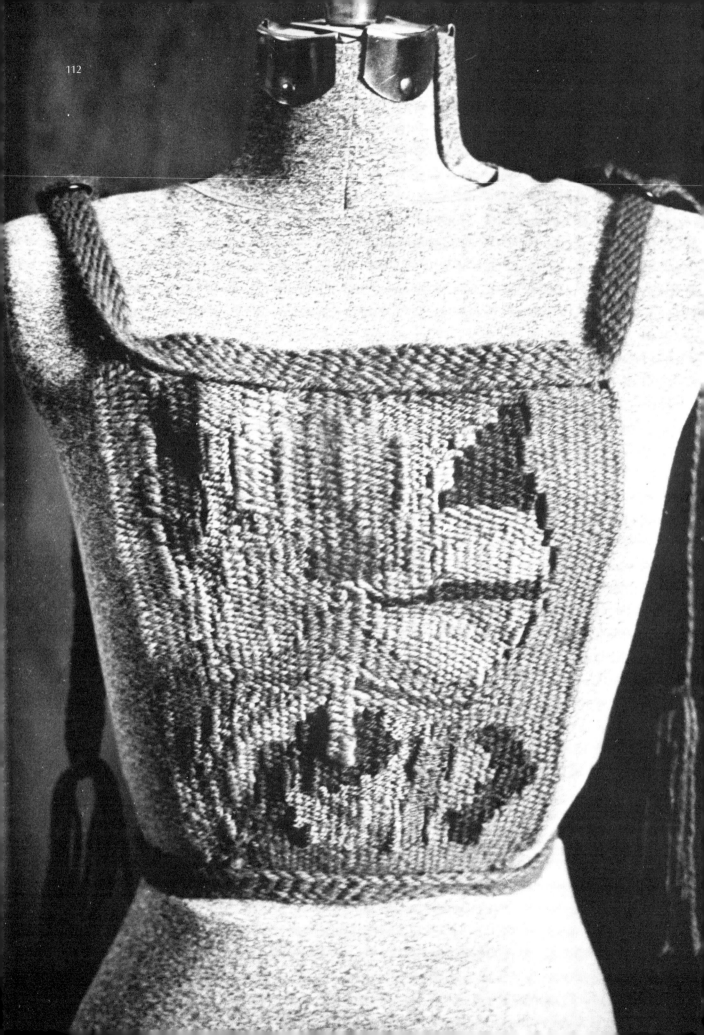

Halters

The versatility of some objects is illustrated by a woman's halter (Figure 112), which may also be used as a man's holster-pocket (Figure 113). When properly lined, this form makes an excellent and convenient costume accessory for a young man. The tapestry-woven halter has long bands of finger weaving which can be used to tie it to the body. It was designed to be worn over a simple garment. A similar-shaped form may also be made for a young child and literally used as a halter.

A halter may also be used as a shoulder bag (Figures 114 and 115), and it even functions as a ski bonnet (Figure 116, p. 68).

113

114

115

116

The simple halter in Figure 117 was constructed of two finger-woven shaped pieces with fringe. Parts of the halter are attached with wrapping, and fringed ends were grouped and wrapped or terminated with pencil sea urchin shells.

The finger-woven halter in Figure 118 is composed of four sections which were attached at their sides and were trimmed with narrow bands that are also finger woven. Figure 119 gives a close-up detail view of the weaving and the attached band.

117

118

119

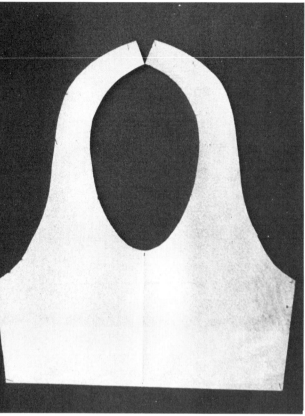

Vests and Boleros

The pattern for the man's buttonless vest in Figure 120 has an opening at the top which allows for its adjustment around the neck and for shoulder fitting. You can close the top with snaps or hook and eye. If you prefer slipping the vest over your head, the top can be sewn together after fitting, thus turning the vest into a pullover.

In Figure 121 the finished weaving is being taken off the loom. The woven front was then attached to a wool-covered wide belting and secured with Velcra fastenings. A stretchable knit back is another possibility for the pullover version. (Figure 122.)

122

In Vinnie Hinz's two-piece bolero vest, both sides were planned and woven at the same time for uniformity. (Figures 123 and 124.) This bolero is designed to have a woven front and a knit or leather back. Note the radiation of the warp threads on the pin loom in Figure 123. Many commercial dressmaker patterns are available for vests and boleros.

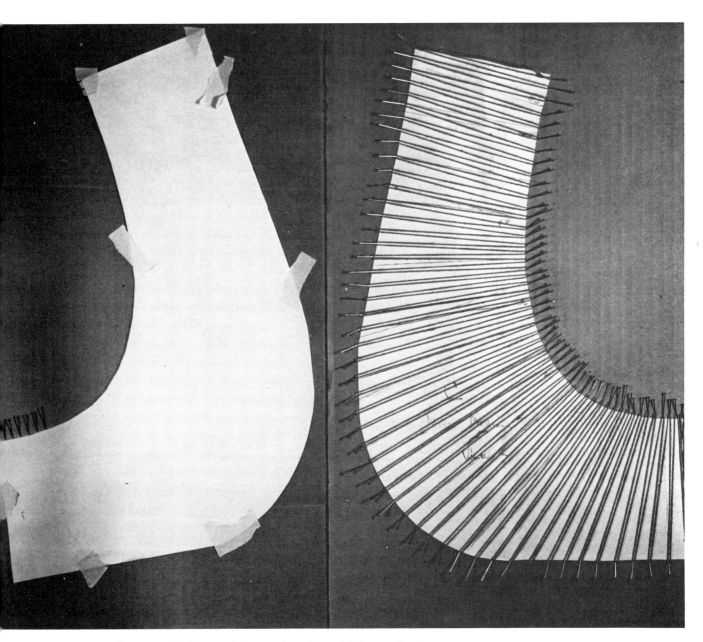

123. The pattern is shown and the warping of one side is completed.

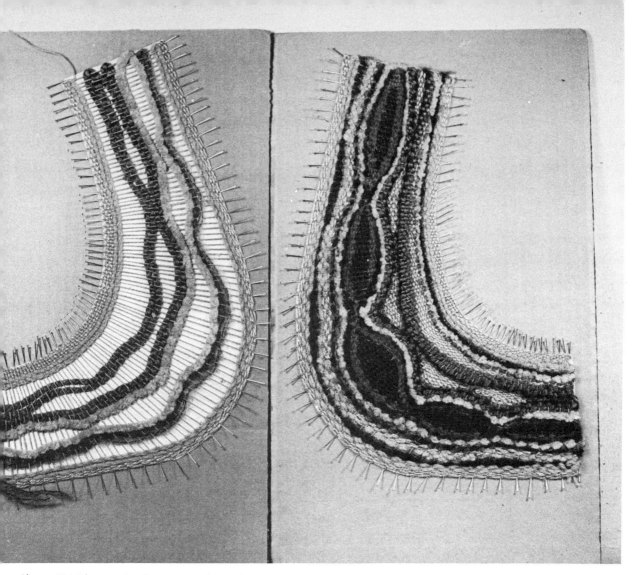

Above: 124. The weaving in progress shows the distribution of the heavy threads.

Below, left: 125. The vest is modeled by Anita Allen.

Below, right: 126. The finished vest was attached to a leather back trimmed with crochet edge.

127. The vest was designed and woven by Kathy Chesness.

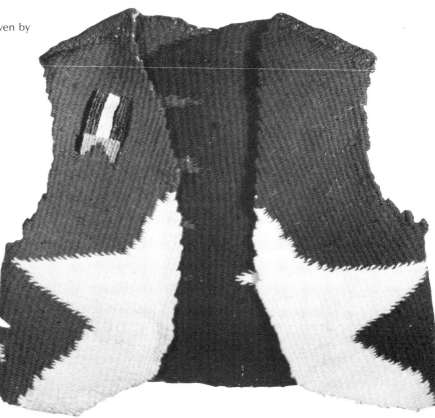

128

The centennial red-white-and-blue bolero vest in Figures 127 and 128 was woven in heavy wool on linen warp, and the inset slit tapestry emblem with a synthetic raffia. The pattern was all one piece and necessitated the folding back of the sides and sewing at the shoulders to complete the form. (Figure 129 and also see color photo C-14.)

129

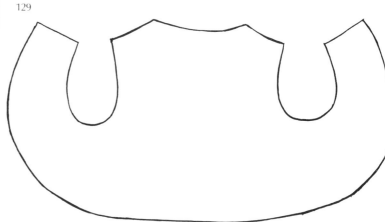

How you might begin the warp for a two-piece vest front is shown in Figure 130. Note the curved line for the pocket opening. The slit is automatically achieved by warping from the top and bottom around the pins at the opening. Drawing on the paper pattern is a good way to indicate design and color change in the weaving pattern.

A bolero vest woven by Diane Ericson is shown in Figures 131 and 132. The weaving was attached to a leather back and has leather fringe trimming. Textural interest is added by a wide variety of yarns and weaves as well as the many metal found objects, such as rusty nails and coins, which contribute to the total effect. Another metal object used on the jacket is the insignia of the San Diego Water Company. In the back view of the vest, note the fringe with long center extensions that were wrapped in colors relating to the front of the garment.

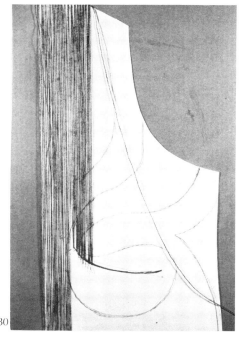

130

Below: 131 and 132. The vest is modeled by Adelina Esquivel.

Capes and Ponchos

Capes and ponchos are some of the larger-scale projects you can make with needle weaving on cardboard looms and with finger weaving. For the woven capelet of Figure 133 the tapestry technique involved extensive macramé and fringe to complete it. The decorative embellishments consist of wrapped threads, metal pieces and an antique neck clasp.

Figures 134 and 135 show how shaped finger weaving can form the border of a leather cape. The curve is achieved in the process of weaving by tighter beating on the side designated as the inside of the weaving. Through this process it is possible to create a variety of curved and wavy shapes.

135

134

In Figures 136 and 137 the authors model a wine-colored leather cape that was made with vari-colored tapestry woven arm insets. Figure 138 shows the weaving up close.

137

The simple large-scale project in Figure 139 is a one-piece poncho that was woven on a cardboard pin loom with irregular edges and a center opening for slipping it over the head. (See also C-1 in the color section and front cover.) This pictorial tapestry design by Diane Ericson was made of a combination of materials, including leather strips. The numerous textures were achieved through a variety of weights of materials.

139

Jewelry: Pendants, Pins, Earrings, Barrettes and Buckles

If you would like to try your hand at something small and detailed, or if you are curious about an example which incorporates its loom in the finished object, nothing is more rewarding than doing a jewelry piece. You could easily do a pin, a pendant, a bracelet, earrings, a barrette or a buckle.

You might be able to find some of the many prefabricated objects that can be used as frameworks in your workshop gadget drawer. Objects like drapery rings and other hardware are very suitable. However, the challenge of making your own is even more intriguing.

The simplest material to begin with is flexible copper wire; if you combine heavy- and light-gauge metal, you might get a varied frame that is more interesting than one of the same weight. Bend the wire into the desired form, by hand or with fine-nosed pliers, and be sure to include a loop by which to suspend the form if it is to be a pendant. To temper the wire, and thereby make it more rigid, we recommend that you hammer it against a metal surface, preferably an anvil.

A commonly available alternative to flexible copper wire is clothes-hanger wire, which is somewhat more difficult to handle, however. Cut this wire with wire snips or the cutting edge of pliers. Then shape it with the pliers.

141. This pear-shaped pendant was woven with a variety of yarns, including flexible metallic thread, woven over wire framework. (See also C-9.)

140. This pendant has a shaped copper wire framework. The loop for the chain and the overlapping spiral shape are part of the one-piece copper form on which the weaving was done. (See also C-8 in the color section.)

The wire framework may remain exposed in places and be an integral part of your design. If you wish to cover it, wind yarn around the basic frame before warping. This also provides a secure nonslip surface for the warp threads. Attach the warp to the wire framework by looping it back and forth, arranging it in any manner which relates to the general shape of the object. Thin wire is suitable for the warp and should give the object extra rigidity. You can make the entire object out of wire if you select material thin enough and flexible enough to work with. In addition to many different metallic colors, wires are now available plastic-coated in a wide selection of hues. Telephone wire is especially effective.

Small jewelry and accessory objects can easily be finished off with commercial findings such as pin backs and earring screws. You should note that many small projects require preplanning and some call for a built-in device for attaching.

143. Anita Allen models a pendant in metallic threads.

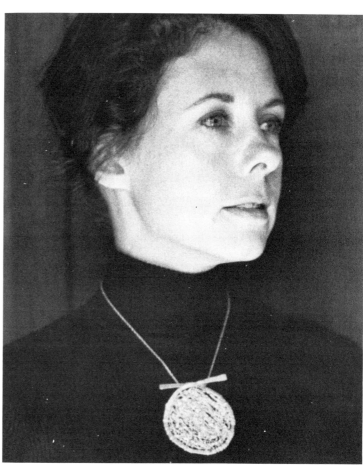

142. The woven wire pendant shows a simple over-and-under tabby weave around the heavier wire frame. Made with black and silver wires, it is 3 inches wide.

Woven jewelry is novel and has much potential — there is no limit to its variety. Objects may be small or large, delicate or bold, but no matter what impression you intend to achieve with your jewelry, remember that it is often seen at close hand and carefully scrutinized by its admirers; therefore it should be as carefully crafted as you can possibly make it.

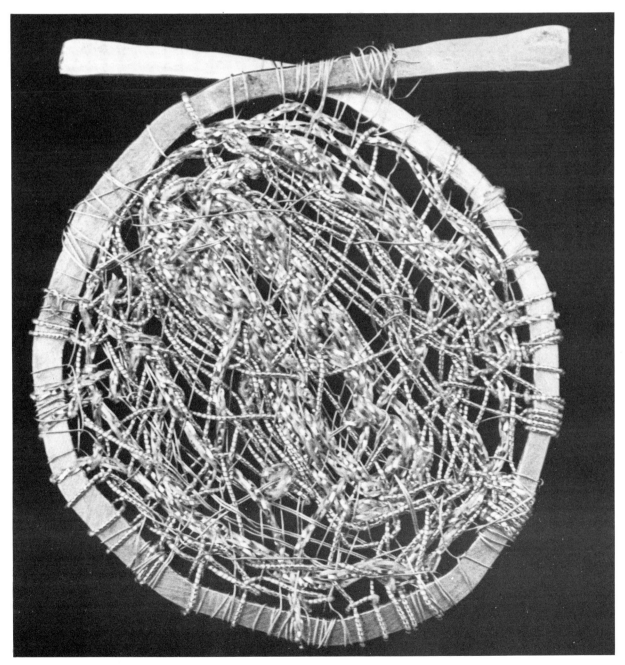

144. A close-up of the pendant in Figure 143 shows how it is woven with silver threads on a one-piece bent and hammered framework.

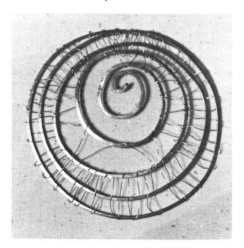

Bent brass wire, with finer flexible wire stretched across various areas, becomes a shaped warp upon which various threads are interwoven, as shown in Figures 146 and 147. (See also color photo C-3.) The textures of smooth metal and fuzzy yarn work well together to create unique woven jewelry. The framework, which actually is the loom, remains an integral, decorative, as well as structural, part of the object.

Similarly, in the pendant of Figure 148, the silver wire frame or armature becomes the skeleton or loom for the weaving. Colored plastic-coated wire was used for the weaving. (See C-2 in the color section.)

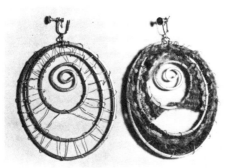

146. Before and after: an earring in progress and the finished example.

147

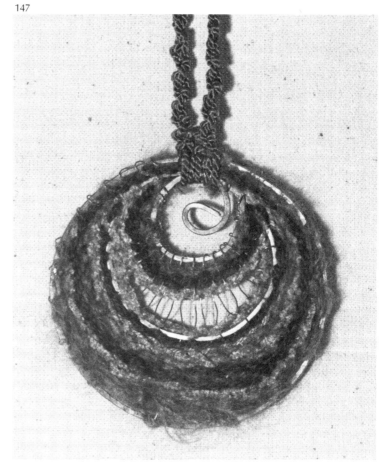

84

149

150

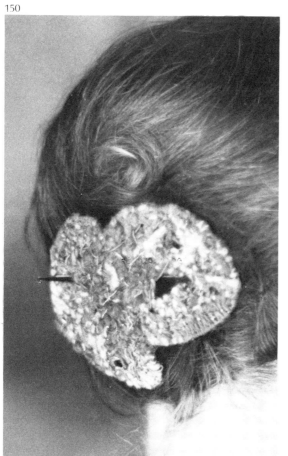

151

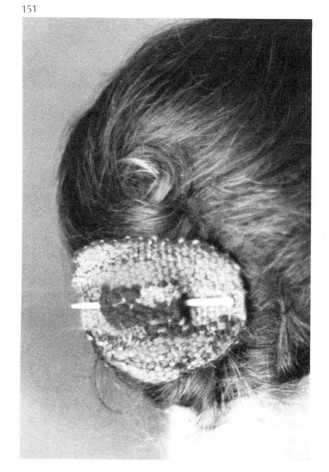

Barrettes can also be woven on metal-wire framework. The intricate overstitching of weft threads gives the examples in Figures 149 and 150 a nonwoven look. Openings have been left for a large hairpin.

The barrette shown in Figure 151 was woven on a pin loom. The slit-tapestry technique was used to allow for hairpins.

In Figure 152, note that the barrette woven with the slit-tapestry technique provides openings for metal hairpins. Wrapped threads add a decorative element to the design, which is also enhanced by bent and hammered pins with yarn heads. (See also color photos C-4 and C-5.)

Some other related projects are pins and buckles. The 2-inch-wide circular pin in Figure 153 has dangling strips. Made on a pin loom, it combines metallic threads with other yarns.

The hair ornament or pin in Figure 154 on the next page features stitching over the needle weaving.

In Figures 155, 156 and 157 (pp. 88 and 89) the three examples of belt buckles are on rigid wire frameworks. Note the variety in the weaving and the use of leather and plastic strips combined with yarn warps.

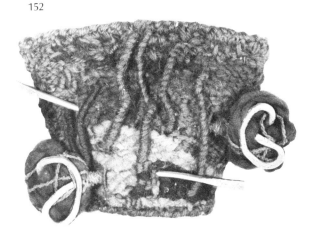

152

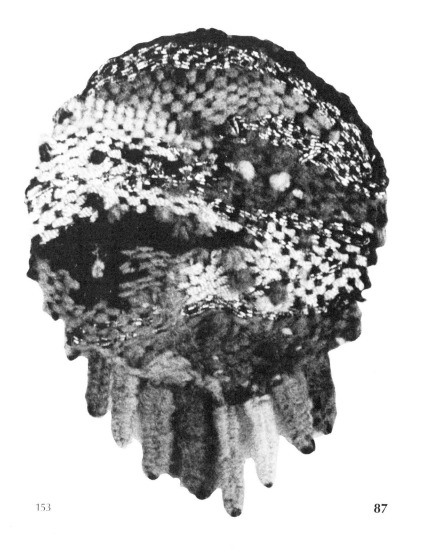

153

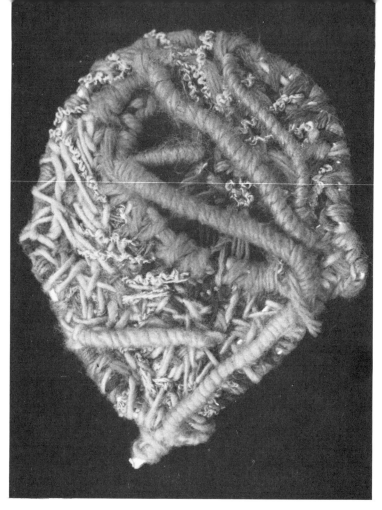

154

155

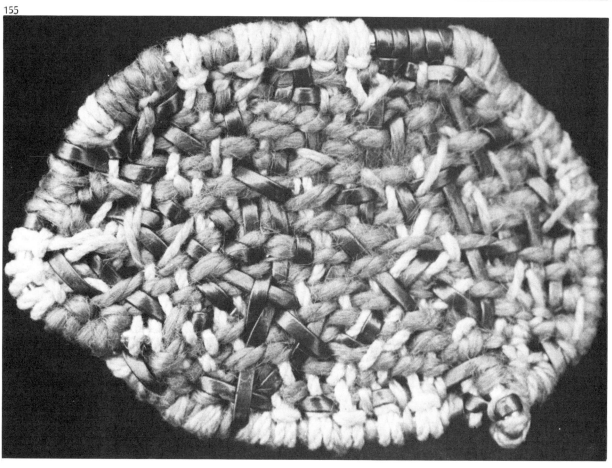

157

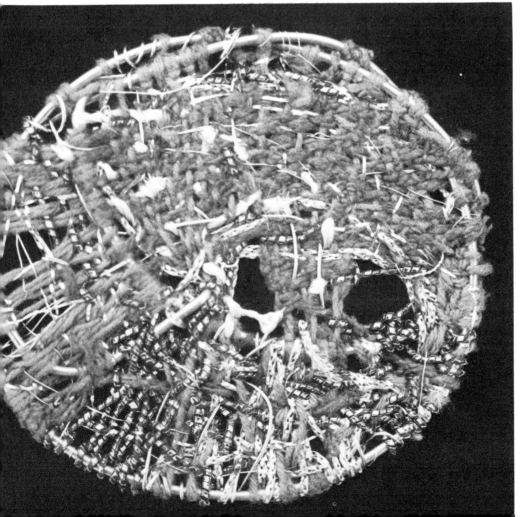

158

Ties and Belts

One of the simplest things you can make in finger weaving is a necktie. The ones by Ellen Anderson in Figure 158 demonstrate two designs achieved by two ways of weaving — straight and chevron patterns. The stripe was created by a symmetrical arrangement of the threads and was woven with an extra thread as weft. The chevron is woven from the center out to both sides.

In the finger-woven chevron belt of Figure 160, a diamond pattern was woven in the center. The piece was woven from the middle of the threads to one end, and then begun again at the center and woven to the opposite end. Three-strand braiding and added beads finish off the ends.

The belt in Figure 161 has pendant forms that combine a variety of techniques. The waist section was finger-woven and attached to the hanging sections with wrapped warps. The sides are meant to be stitched to pants or a skirt, creating the effect of decorative panels.

Below, left: 159. A close-up larger detail of the chevron tie in Figure 158.

160

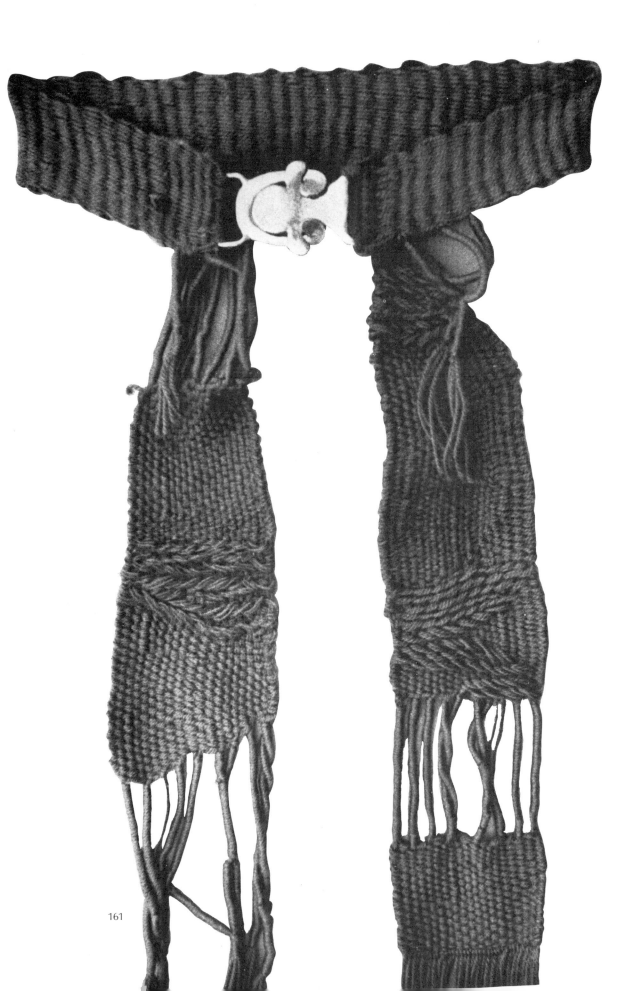

161

162

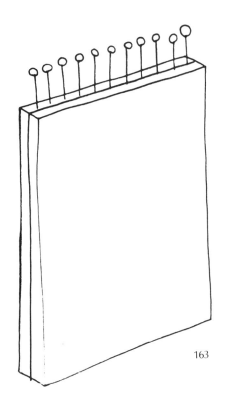

163

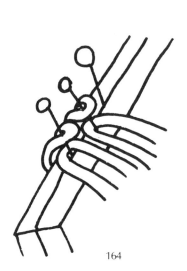

164

165

Three-Dimensional Shaped Weaving

We have described shaped weaving done with the fingers and on different kinds of two-dimensional looms. Although these weavings are designed to conform to the body, they are not constructed upon it or upon similar shaped objects such as mannequins. They are created flat, unlike the three-dimensional projects that are described in this last section.

Many forms are available as bases for three-dimensional constructions: dressmaker dummies, hat and wig forms, mannequins, shoe lasts and other devices which conform to the body are suitable. It is possible to construct an entire form-fitting garment or accessory on a three-dimensional form and remove it as a completed object, without ever encountering the need for seams. Some projects, however, must have openings so that they can be put on easily. These may be constructed as side, front or back openings for a variety of closures, such as buttons, hooks or zippers. Sometimes, laced, wrapped and braided ties are effective.

The procedure for warping and weaving in three-dimensional construction is similar to what you have already done, with extra consideration being given to the form upon which the object is being made. Some objects you can make with a continuous warp and remove; others will require various directional sections.

The one-piece purse on the next page was created on a double-thickness cardboard shape (Figure 162) which held the pins for the warp threads. (See Figure 163.) The warp was tied to the bottom corner of the cardboard and attached around the pins at the top. (Figure 164.) The thread goes up and around the pin head, down the same side, then under the cardboard and up the other side and around the same pin. (Figure 165.) It then proceeds back to the first side and continues in the same manner until it has been attached to all the pins from both sides. The end of warp is pinned to the opposite bottom corner. Weaving is done with needle and wool or other resilient yarn, starting at the bottom and continuing around the form until the top is reached. (Figure 166.) When the pins are removed, the completed seamless one-piece envelope purse is ready to be lined, attached to the top clasp and trimmed as desired. The purse shown here has an ornamental silver buckle and fringe ends tied on to the bottom.

166

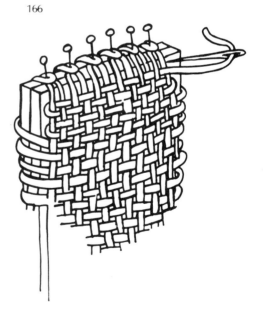

167

94

A thicker envelope bag can be created with horizontal warping, as shown in Figures 168, 169 and 170. The warp, which is attached by a pin, began at the bottom corner and was wrapped continuously around three layers of cardboard. Spacing was controlled by tension on the warp thread and was equalized in the course of weaving. The illustrations of this example in progress show how a pattern may be moved around as various color areas are added. As the weaving continued, tension was increased, and when the weaving became too tight for easy working, one layer of the cardboard was slipped out to release the tension. Once the weaving was completed, the rest of the cardboard was removed. Loose ends of the beginning and ending of each color could be left as long as they all appeared on the working side. When the object was turned inside out, the outside had a finished appearance.

168. Front view of the envelope bag in progress.

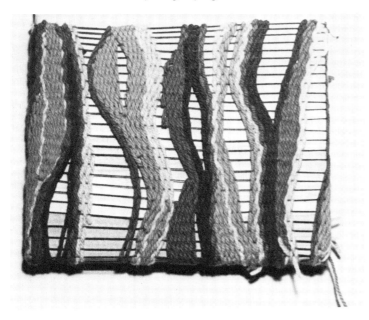

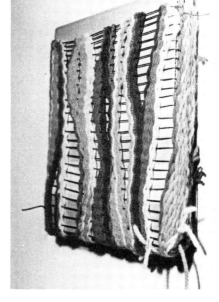

170. Side view.

169. Bottom view.

The completed one-piece envelope form, designed for multipurpose use by Vinnie Hinz, is shown in Figure 171. This shape may be finished with a zipper and straps for a shoulder bag, or may function as a pouch, or even a hat as demonstrated in Figures 172, 173, 174 and 175, which show a variety of ways to wear the hat.

172

173

174

174 and 175. The woven hat takes on
numerous shapes.

175

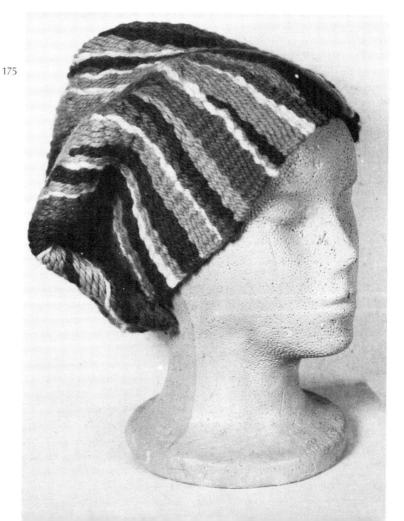

Some of the varieties of three-dimensional forms on which to do your weaving are shown in Figures 176, 177 and 178. In Figure 176, the weaving is being done on a Styrofoam mold. Neckpieces or chokers, headbands and hats are the kinds of objects you can make on this form.

Note the continuous round weaving that is possible on a tube form such as the one shown in Figure 177. Armbands, cuffs, wristbands and bracelets may be made this way.

In Figure 178 the weaving is being done on a wooden hat block. The shape of the object depicted in this illustration would make an excellent hair ornament. Slip the ponytail or bun through the center opening for a unique coiffure.

177

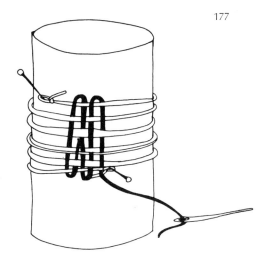

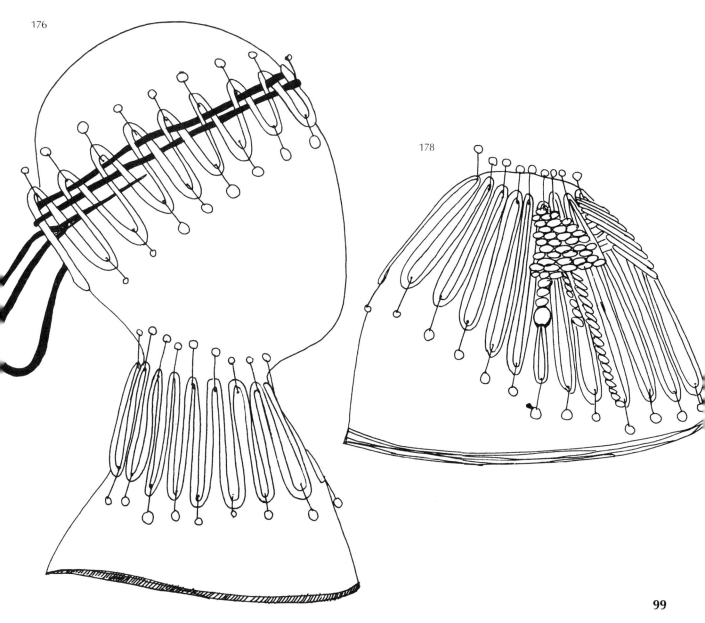

176

178

179

180

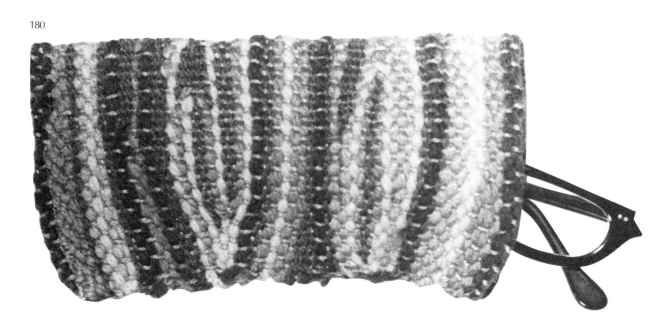

The glasses holders in Figures 179 and 180 were made out of a flat woven shape folded to create a slip case. the forms were padded and lined and then sewn together at the bottom and sides. You can make the case with the same method used for the envelope bag and hat. (See Figures 168–170.)

The use of natural materials and the concept of basket weaving are applied extensions of the shaped weaving technique. In Figure 181, the back-pack woven and modeled by Diane Ericson is made of shaped twigs, cane and bark and has a leather flap closure. In working with cane, reed, and other pliable materials which may be shaped in many ways, you have the opportunity to explore the construction of containers and other forms which may be used as accessories. The shape may be dictated by the natural material, as in the case of the twigs which conform to the back in the back-pack illustrated.

181

You can construct an entire garment or some other form by weaving the separate sections on similar looms of different sizes. The tubes of various length and circumference depicted in Figure 182 were used to construct a stuffed doll (Figure 183) with the pin loom technique.

We end with this example in order to suggest the numerous objects other than wearable garments or clothing accessories that you can make with techniques described in Part I of this book. It might be a point of departure for you, leading you to think about making furnishings, soft sculpture and other decorative objects or works of art.

Continue to experiment with the principles and techniques you have learned. They may inspire you to work with a variety of materials other than fibers and bring you into the realm of basket weaving or other three-dimensional forms. Since our concern was with objects for dress, we have not shown examples of these other applications, but we trusted that the creative reader would imaginatively extend what we have presented in his own personal way.

We wish you many happy hours with the media and techniques of needle weaving on cardboard looms and finger weaving, and with all the original interpretations you will develop.

182

About The Authors

Nik Krevitsky, artist, educator and author, is a recognized leader in the field of crafts. An active designer-craftsman as well as painter, he has exhibited throughout the United States and in several foreign countries. He is best known for his work in fibers and his stitcheries have been seen in many invitational shows and collections, among them the prestigious OBJECTS: USA, the Johnson Collection and a one-man exhibition at the Smithsonian Institution.

As an influential participant and officer in several professional art and craft organizations, Nik Krevitsky has contributed to the growing interest in and development of art education today. His recent books *Batik: Art and Craft* and *Stitchery: Art and Craft* were published by Van Nostrand Reinhold.

Nik Krevitsky has taught and conducted workshops in many universities and is currently Director of Art and the Educational Materials Center, Tucson Public Schools, in Tucson, Arizona.

Lois Ericson is a practicing craftswoman in the field of fibers, having learned hand arts from her mother in the true Swedish tradition. Her recent interest in weaving, after many years of involvement in other fiber techniques, led to innovation in simple methods of achieving shaped forms. With this exploration she has incorporated macramé, crochet, wrapping and other methods.

Affiliated with the Contemporary Handweavers of San Francisco and the Sacramento Weavers Guild, Lois Ericson conducts workshops in fibers and exhibits and produces woven garments in addition to running a busy household in Tahoe City, California.

Together the authors have developed this book out of a mutual interest in the potential of the "shaped weaving" concept, with an awareness that there has not been enough available material to show those who are interested in this area how to get started.

Bibliography

Albers, Anni. *On Weaving.* Middletown, Connecticut: Wesleyan University Press, 1965.

Alexander, Marthann. *Simple Weaving.* New York: Taplinger Publishing Co., 1969.

Bevlin, Marjorie Elliott. *Design Through Discovery.* New York: Holt, Rinehart and Winston, Inc., 1970.

Black, Mary E. *New Key to Weaving.* Milwaukee, Wisconsin: The Bruce Publishing Co., 1957.

Blumenau, Lili. *The Art and Craft of Hand Weaving.* New York: Crown Publishers, Inc., 1955.

Hartung, Rolf. *Creative Textile Design: Thread and Fabric.* New York: Van Nostrand Reinhold Co., 1963.

Harvey, Virginia I. *Macramé: The Art of Creative Knotting.* New York: Van Nostrand Reinhold Co., 1968.

Krevitsky, Nik. *Stitchery: Art and Craft.* New York: Van Nostrand Reinhold Co., 1966.

Lind, Vibeke. *Practical Modern Crochet.* New York: Van Nostrand Reinhold Co., 1973.

Moseley, Spencer; Johnson, Pauline; and Koenig, Hazel. *Crafts Design, an Illustrated Guide.* Belmont, California: Wadsworth Publishing Co., 1962.

Phillips, Mary Walker. *Creative Knitting: A New Art Form.* New York: Van Nostrand Reinhold Co., 1971.

Rainey, Sarita. *Weaving Without a Loom.* Worcester, Massachusetts: Davis Publications, Inc., 1966.

Thorpe, Azalea Stuart and Larsen, Jack Lenor. *Elements of Weaving.* New York: Doubleday, 1967.

Willcox, Donald J. *Techniques of Rya Knotting.* New York: Van Nostrand Reinhold Co., 1971.

Wilson, Jean. *Weaving Is for Anyone.* New York: Van Nostrand Reinhold Co., 1967.